MODERN HUMANITIES RESEARCH ASSOCIATION
NEW TRANSLATIONS
VOLUME 5

GENERAL EDITOR
ALISON FINCH

ITALIAN EDITOR
MARK DAVIE

RUSTICO FILIPPI
THE ART OF INSULT

TRANSLATED BY
FABIAN ALFIE

Rustico Filippi

The Art of Insult

Translated by
Fabian Alfie

Modern Humanities Research Association
2014

Published by

The Modern Humanities Research Association,
Salisbury House
Station Road
Cambridge CB1 2LA
United Kingdom

© The Modern Humanities Research Association, 2014

Fabian Alfie has asserted his right under the Copyright, Designs and Patents Act 1988 to be identified as the author of this work. Parts of this work may be reproduced as permitted under legal provisions for fair dealing (or fair use) for the purposes of research, private study, criticism, or review, or when a relevant collective licensing agreement is in place. All other reproduction requires the written permission of the copyright holder who may be contacted at rights@mhra.org.uk.

First published 2014

ISBN 978-1-78188-157-6

www.translations.mhra.org.uk

CONTENTS

Acknowledgements	vi
Introduction	1
Bibliography	11
Rustico Filippi	18
Iacopo da Lèona	139
Mino da Colle	157
Niccola Muscia of Siena	165
Iacomo de' Tolomei Nicknamed 'il graffione' ('The Lacerator')	175
Dante's *tenzone* with Forese Donati	181

ACKNOWLEDGEMENTS

I would like to acknowledge the following people for their feedback and assistance in revising the translations of Rustico Filippi: Mary E. Graham, David Klanderman, Nicolino Applauso, and Maria Alfie. I would like to extend special thanks to Mark Davie for his meticulous readings and insightful suggestions.

INTRODUCTION

RUSTICO FILIPPI NICKNAMED 'IL BARBUTO'
(c. 1230–1240/c. 1295–1299)

The Art of Insult

Nowadays it may be difficult to talk about the art of insult. Insult is typically viewed as a spontaneous utterance inspired by anger, hatred, or contempt; such a perspective has little room for artfulness or study. The closest comparison might be to professional comics and rappers who engage in insult as part of their craft. Yet in the Middle Ages, insult literally became an art form. Criminals who were convicted in absentia risked having their likenesses and crimes depicted in murals on public buildings. Slanderous rhymes appear in historical chronicles, such as those by Salimbene de Adam and Dino Compagni. Insult was also a key part of literature, and it served a social function. Literary insult enforced ethics by publicly chastising the immoral, and as such it had an established set of rhetorical and stylistic rules. It was supposed to treat low matters with low language, so therefore offensive topics, expressions, and lexicon were required of it. Insulting poetry, in particular, was central to the medieval literary tradition, and it had its own masterful authors. Although many people composed insulting verse, perhaps the father of literary derision in Italy was Rustico Filippi. Through numerous sonnets Rustico Filippi explored the rhetorical and stylistic possibilities of insulting poetry. He put into practice the rhetorical teachings, and demonstrated how the sonnet form, which had previously only been used for amorous material, could be a vehicle for social and political satire. Rustico inspired numerous imitators including the young Dante Alighieri, the author of the *Divine Comedy*.

Little is known about Rustico Filippi's life. He may have born into a non-noble Florentine family between 1230 and 1240. During his lifetime he was also known by the nickname, 'il barbuto' (the bearded man). In the 1260s, Dante's teacher Brunetto Latini dedicated the lengthy poem *Favolello* to Filippi, writing: 'Now, what I think or say, / I turn to you, my friend / Rustico di Filippo' ('Or, che ch'i' penso o dico, / A te mi torno amico, / Rustico di Filippo', vv. 135–38). Most of the biographical information about Filippi has been deduced from city archives relating to his sons. Lapus Rustici, 'the son of Rustico, of the neighborhood of Santa Maria' ('filius Rustechi, populi sancte Marie in campo'), joined the guild of silk in 1286; the city archive indicates that Rustico lived in the area around the church of Santa Maria Novella. In a document dated 23–30 January 1299, the scribe refers to another son Lippus as 'formerly of Rustico Filippi' ('Lippus quondam Rustici Filippi'). Following scribal procedures at the time, the word 'formerly' ('quondam') indicates that Rustico had died within the preceding five years. Rustico left a corpus of fifty-nine sonnets, almost evenly divided between love poems (twenty-nine) and comic verse (thirty). All of his sonnets except one are contained in the Florentine manuscript Vatican Latin 3793, a compendium of Florentine poetry of the third quarter of the thirteenth century; only two of the sonnets from that manuscript are also found in any other medieval codices.[1] Vatican Latin 3793 is written in *mercantesca*, a handwriting developed by merchants for commerce and accounting. The manuscript indicates Rustico to have been an important member of the literary generation just preceding Dante.

Rustico lived through tumultuous decades for Italy and the Florentine Republic. The thirteenth century witnessed great ideological struggles between the popes and emperors for political supremacy in Europe. When Emperor Frederick II died in Apulia in 1250, the pro-imperial forces, known as Ghibellines, were ascendant in Italy. At the battle of Montaperti in 1260 the Tuscan Ghibellines defeated the Florentine Guelphs (pro-papal forces). Afterwards, the popes undercut the Ghibellines by annulling all debts owed to Ghibellines; many pro-imperial bankers switched sides rather than forfeit their earnings. The popes also installed the French royal Charles I of Anjou to the vacated throne of Naples with the hopes that he would defeat Frederick's son Manfred. At the battle of Benevento in 1266, the fortunes of the Guelphs and Ghibellines were reversed; the Guelphs defeated the Ghibellines, and Manfred, the heir to Frederick, was killed. With the defeat and beheading of Conradin, Frederick's grandson, at the battle of Tagliacozzo in 1268, the Ghibellines' hopes for restoration were crushed. After 1268, Tuscany and central Italy remained overwhelmingly Guelph, although battles with the Ghibellines would take place for decades afterwards.

Despite the desperation of the political context, the economies of the Italian communes flourished. Cities specialized in trade and manufacturing, and people earned unheard-of amounts of wealth through money lending. Leading the other cities was Florence, whose population quintupled throughout the thirteenth century. As the economy grew, wealthy nobles moved to the city, bringing with them their rents from the countryside; money flowed into the cities, therefore, which then capitalized new enterprises, generating an ever-expanding market. Non-noble merchants became wealthy and intermarried with the established nobility forming a new class of magnates; Rustico seems to have belonged to the merchants, and the primary manuscript containing his verse may have originated

---

[1] Sonnet 59A is also found in Magliabechiano VII 1040 of the Central Library of Florence; IX. it. 529 of the Marciano Library of Venice; and Chigiano L. VIII. 305 of the Vatican Library. Sonnet 34 is found in Vatican Latin 3214.

in that socio-cultural context as well. But the economic changes of the cities far outpaced their culture. Urban nobles retained the medieval mindset of blood feuds and the inferiority of non-nobles. They believed that trade and earnings through interest were beneath a nobleman — even while earning vast amounts of money doing so. Violence abounded, and the city governments struggled to provide security. Meanwhile the rising wealth caused people to behave in unacceptable ways. One way to reinforce traditional, ethical behavior was insult, the public exposure of immorality.

For centuries, medieval theorists had proposed an all-inclusive definition of literature as either praise (*laus*) or blame (*vituperatio*). Tragedies inspired readers to praise laudable individuals, and conversely, comedies held blameworthy people up for ridicule and scorn. In his commentary on Aristotle, Averroes (1126–1198) emphasized that all literature consisted of either the praise of the virtuous or the blame of the wicked; Averroes' perspective was first introduced into Europe through the translation of his works by Hermann the German, after which it became commonplace. Thus, for centuries insult was part and parcel of the poetics of blame. In his *Ars versificatoria* (c. 1175) Matthew of Vendôme explained that the very descriptions of characters conveyed the author's praise or reprehension. In his treatise Matthew provided one example of blame, the portrait of the old hag Beroë (I, 58). Over the course of some forty-five verses, he enumerates her nauseating physical state, her stench, filth, parasites, and bodily secretions. Such revolting language, labeled as *feditas*, was not unique to Matthew's portrait of Beroë, but rather was intrinsic to medieval satiric literature. Medieval literary theorists repeated the classical definition of satire as an ethical art dedicated to the reprehension of vice. They said that the genre of satire was named after satyrs; just as satyrs are nude, so too are satires nude in so far as they employ blunt language.

Rustico's poetic corpus embodies the praise / blame dichotomy of the age. Like numerous other thirteenth-century Italian poets he composed love literature that praised a beloved woman. However, in the Italian vernacular tradition, no one had fully explored the poetry of blame before Rustico. In the *Favolello*, Brunetto Latini asked Rustico to send examples of his 'new' style of writing: 'And this writing which I send to you / is the reason, and I ask / that it may please you to dictate / and to send to me / some of your latest poetry' ('E ciò che scritto mando, / È cagione, e dimando, / Che ti piaccia dittare / E me scritto mandare / Del tuo trovato adesso', vv. 149–53). Additionally, in the commentary to Francesco da Barberino's *Documenti d'Amore* (c. 1317) Rustico Filippi is mentioned. The commentator numbers the late Rustico among those who excoriated women instead of praising them ('Quid enim Rusticus barbutus et alij quidam, laudis ex vituperiis per eos impintis contra dominas reportarunt'). Therefore, the two documents indicate that Rustico's contemporaries considered him to have innovated in vernacular poetry with his insulting sonnets.

In his poetry Rustico demonstrates awareness of Matthew of Vendôme's literary ideas. In one sonnet he insults and abuses an old woman in the manner of Matthew's description of Beroë. Filippi describes her smell as being so foul that people plug their noses and flee. In other sonnets, he presents individuals following Matthew's teaching about negative descriptions. He portrays some men as so fat that they cause their horses to faint and ships to sink; he depicts others as so ugly that God Himself must have wanted to make a new miracle when they were conceived. Some people are so smelly that they rival the stench of caged lions or even tombs. Rustico's poetry has been described as a series of caricatures: they are third-person descriptions of the individuals in which the figure of the poet is virtually absent. Instead, he lets the seemingly objective descriptions of his subjects communicate his disdain to his readers. At times, the people's immorality is apparent, while in others it is not so clear. In fact, without historical corroboration about some of them, we can only guess at the accuracy of the poet's opinions of them.

The targets of many of Rustico's caricatures are adulterous women. He portrays several of them in bluntly sexual terms — even recalling when he had sex with one on the floor of a stall. He mentions another young woman's sudden thinness, possibly the result of an illicit abortion. Rustico did not develop his misogynistic subject matter *ex nihilo*, but rather was part of a centuries-long tradition. Probably the most influential misogynistic work of the Middle Ages was Jerome's *Adversus Jovinianum*, an extreme diatribe indebted to the classical satirists like Juvenal, Horace and Ovid. In it, Jerome enumerates women's faults and emphasized their physical repulsiveness with the purpose of enforcing monastic celibacy. Other Church Fathers, like Augustine, followed suit, inspiring an on-going literary movement of misogynistic invectives containing horrendous descriptions of women's bodies and their mean-spirited and lustful attitudes, and the abhorrence of sexual activities. By the thirteenth century, numerous such texts existed, a literary practice that probably inspired Matthew of Vendôme's depiction of Beroë. As the citation from the commentary on Francesco da Barberino's *Documenti d'Amore* indicates, however, Rustico made a reputation for himself as a misogynistic writer. He may have been responsible for the translation of the misogynistic trope into the Italian vernacular from Latin. The literary giant of the age, Guittone d'Arezzo (1235–1294), suggested in a *canzone* the novelty of misogynistic writings in the vernacular when he defended women against those poets who slander them ('Ahi lasso, chi li boni e li malvagi'). Indeed, the cultural basis for medieval misogyny stands out given Rustico's historical context. He did not compose such poems in the tranquility of a monastery, but amid the bustle of a crowded urban commune. As the economy flourished and women took on increasing social and economic power, Rustico's poetry served to reinforce the traditional teachings about women's roles and very natures.

For instance, many editors of Filippi's verse doubt the ascription of sonnet 30 to him, the sole poem in his corpus not found in the Vatican Latin 3793 manuscript (instead, Vatican Urbinate 697). The fifteenth-century manuscript identifies its author as 'Rustico barbuto', but the poem appears in a corrupted form. In that poem Rustico states that when his lady wants to please him with food, she takes the rheum off her eyelids, peels the crust from her scabies, and fills the bowl with excrement from the cesspool. Scholars of the Middle Ages are beginning to explore the medieval attitudes toward the human body, arguing that its excreta and effluvia were the direct result of sinfulness.[2] This was particularly true of female bodies, about which menstrual blood and childbirth only underscored their fallen nature.[3] As in sonnet 30, Rustico's representations of dripping, leaking, smelly human bodies — that is to say, his caricatures of reprehensible individuals — conform to the conclusions of modern-day scholars. His portraits are not of spiritual beings, but of fleshy creatures subject to the bodily decay that is the result of human vice. The woman of sonnet 30 is not one of the rarefied ladies of medieval love poetry, but a producer of filth and the fodder for parasites. She is, in short, symbolic of the human body that all people should reject in favor of the soul, according to Christian ascetic tradition.

In addition to his misogynistic verse, a number of Rustico's comic poems are political satires. Rustico, a Ghibelline, mentions political figures like Charles I, the papacy, and the Holy Roman Empire. He also refers to the struggles between the Guelphs and Ghibellines in the 1260s and 70s, thereby providing a general date for his literary activities. In one sonnet he insults the Florentine Ghibellines, calling them cowards because they fled after the Guelph victory at Benevento in 1266. But now that the danger has passed they can return safely to Florence and start fighting the war again. He explains that none of the Ghibellines can threaten the Guelphs with excommunication, a sarcastic reference to the popes' political use of expulsion from the Church. In other sonnets he satirizes a fellow Ghibelline, Fastello, whose arrogant boasting reflects poorly on the political party as a whole. Thus, Filippi's poetry constitutes an early development in the evolution of Italian political verse. Subsequent writers such as Folgore da San Gimignano (ca. 1270-ca. 1332) and Pietro dei Faitinelli (ca. 1280-1349) demonstrated Rustico's influence in their own political verse. Additionally, Rustico set the example for probably the most important political writer of the age, Dante Alighieri.

The language in Filippi's comic poems is striking. He utilizes low linguistic registers, crass obscenities, coarse allusions, harsh phonetics, and vivid imagery. Filippi uses direct language to speak of sexual matters, the body and its functions,

---

[2] Martha Bayless, *Sex and Filth in Medieval Culture: The Devil in the Latrine* (New York, London: Routledge, 2012): xviii.
[3] Susan Signe Morrison, *Excrement in the Late Middle Ages: Sacred Filth and Chaucer's Fecopoetics* (New York: Palgrave MacMillan, 2008): 45. See also Alexandra Cuffel, *Gendering Disgust in Medieval Religious Polemic* (Notre Dame IN: University of Notre Dame Press, 2007): 6.

and immoral activities. Rustico allows his readers to see — often smell — his characters (they don't smell good). His use of blunt, bawdy lexicon was required by the stylistic conventions established by medieval literary theorists. Style, it was said, needed to conform to the subject matter it treated, and reprehensible people demanded low language. He also employed some colloquial expressions, slang, and suggestive allusions that escape our current understanding, and require us to make educated guesses. Of course, Rustico's language made his insulting poems appear that much more offensive. While his love literature uses terms derived from the Provençal and Sicilian schools of poetry, his comic verse approximates the Florentine vernacular. It is as if his comic poetry thrusts the reader into the crowded, bustling streets of late thirteenth-century Italy.

Rustico had a profound impact on Italian literature of the Middle Ages. Other poets of the age, such as Iacopo da Lèona, Mino da Colle, and Niccola Muscia are linked to him, and therefore are included in this volume. The poems of Iacopo and Mino are found in the very same manuscript as Rustico; Niccola Muscia's verse had a different circulation (Vatican Latin Chigiano L.VIII.305 and Vatican Barberiniano Latin 3953), but Rustico mentions him by name. This is not to say that they formed a poetic school because several of them addressed derisive poetry to Rustico Filippi or other individuals; yet it is clear that they learned from the master at the same time that they turned his weapons against him. Iacopo da Lèona composed a sonnet insulting Rustico for alleviating his poverty by acting as highway robber. Like Filippi, Iacopo da Lèona also composed amorous verse with no hint of irony. Mino da Colle wrote vituperative political poetry in the manner of Filippi, as well as love sonnets. The Sienese poet Niccola Muscia may represent the earliest example of homoerotic passion in Italian literature; Muscia was publicly derided for his homosexuality by Rustico Filippi and Iacomo dei Tolomei (whose sole extant sonnet is also in this collection). Finally, two of Filippi's sonnets influenced Dante Alighieri who similarly wrote insulting sonnets to a friend, Forese Donati (d. 1296).[4] In his two poems, Rustico speaks to a cuckolded husband, warning him about a friend, ser Cerbiolin. The addressee of the sonnet, Ghigo, is now so cold — because he is sexually ignored by his wife — that he coughs in the middle of July (vv. 5–6). In Dante's first sonnet to Forese Donati, he accuses his friend of abandoning his marital bed and, echoing Rustico, describes Forese's wife as being cold in August and therefore suffering from a cough (vv. 1–2; 5). In later decades, Giovanni Boccaccio would recall some of

---

[4] The sonnets between Dante and Forese Donati are not found in the same manuscripts as those containing the poetry of Rustico Filippi. The sonnets of the *tenzone* most indebted to Rustico Filippi appear in Chigiano L.VIII.305 (f. 62v), Banco Rari 69 (vv. 8v–9r), and Trivulziano 1058 (ff. 43v–44r). For more information about the codicology of the *tenzone* between Dante and Forese Donati, see Fabian Alfie, *Dante's* Tenzone *with Forese Donati: The Reprehension of Vice* (Toronto: University of Toronto Press, 2011): 124–43.

Rustico's insulting language in his masterpiece *Decameron* (c. 1351) and his anti-feminist diatribe *Corbaccio* (c. 1355–1365).

Even at the end of Rustico's life, Florence's political situation remained difficult. Throughout the 1280s and 90s, the guilds dominated city government, and they strove to rein in the unruly urban magnates. Several restrictive laws were put in place, including the Ordinances of Justice, which prohibited the highest families from office; the Ordinances also required the families to post bond, which would be forfeited in the event of violent offenses. In 1295, the laws were weakened, but the Florentine Guelphs split over how to respond. Led by Vieri de' Cerchi, a non-noble merchant, one faction tried to accommodate the wishes of the guilds; after the turn of the fourteenth century, the pro-Cerchi faction would be labeled the Whites. The other faction, subsequently called Blacks, were led by Corso Donati who hoped to reassert the traditional rights of the nobility to dominate society. The factional strife between the Whites and Blacks resulted in coups and street violence, and figures such as Niccola Muscia, Guido Cavalcanti (d. 1300), and Dante Alighieri were caught up in the turmoil. In 1302, Pope Boniface VIII sided with the Blacks and helped organize their takeover of the city government, which resulted in the exile of the Whites, including Dante. Niccola Muscia's slander of Cavalcanti, a White, may reflect the factionalism of the day because Niccola may have been politically motivated to highlight Cavalcanti's failings. Given the restricted roles of the urban nobility during these decades, the culture debated the importance and value of the aristocracy. Some people, like Dante, defined nobility strictly as an individual's inner virtue. Others applied the Aristotelian definition that inherited honors resulted in greater opportunities to behave in a moral fashion, thereby stressing the importance of noble families. Dante's *tenzone* with Forese Donati, Corso's brother, appears to be a product of the debates about nobility. Both men insult each other's family and implicitly pose the question if they are truly noble. Members of the Donati robbed, and members of the Alighieri earned a living in a manner beneath nobility, money lending. As is the case with Rustico, the insulting poetry of his imitators provides a glimpse into the society and politics of the time when it was written.

It is perhaps ironic that Rustico is best known for his poetics of insult. Fully half of his extant poetic corpus was dedicated to love, and he was a quite capable love poet. The persistence of the noble ethos in thirteenth-century Florence resulted in the translation of courtly love literature from Provençal into Italian. The age saw a flourishing of love poetry composed in the vernacular, particularly in Sicily and, later, Tuscany. Until the end of the thirteenth-century Italian poetry was dominated by traditional tropes of medieval love: the exaltation of the woman, the fear of gossips, the lover's jealousy, and his undying devotion to the woman. All of these elements are present in Rustico's love literature, as well as that composed by Iacopo da Lèona and Mino da Colle. In the place of his insulting third-person caricatures, Rustico composes first-person love poetry. In much of his amorous verse, he expresses the pain he feels by loving the woman, explaining that his great suffering should have caused his death but the god of Love intervened. When he is far from her, he burns. He fears that cruel bystanders will speak of his passion, exposing him to ridicule. He portrays the woman as shining like the planet Venus, or as a being superior to him. Even the language of Rustico's love poetry is different from that of his comic verse. Gone are the native Tuscan terms and expressions, replaced instead with Tuscanized Sicilian and Provençal lexicon. Rustico opts for more learned vocabulary in his love lyrics (e.g., 'allegranza', 'bieltà[te]'), distinct from the humble words having the same meanings in his comic verse (e.g., 'allegrezza', 'bellezza'). Instead of the earthy language of his insults, Rustico depicts a rarefied image of Love, the beloved woman, and himself as a traditional courtly lover all in a straightforward manner. It would be members of the next generation — Guido Guinizzelli, Guido Cavalcanti and Dante — who would transform traditional love literature into the philosophical poetry of the *dolce stil nuovo*. In his guise as a love poet Rustico, rather, was an adherent of the traditional view of passion.

Unlike his more famous contemporary Cecco Angiolieri (*c*. 1260–1312), who also composed derisive verse, Rustico Filippi has never been fully translated into English. Three of his sonnets appear in Dante Gabriel Rossetti's early-twentieth-century translation of Italian medieval literature (sonnets 10, 14, and 17), and in 1974 Joseph Tusiani published two (sonnets 4 and 14 again). Thus, fifty-five of Rustico's poems have never been available to readers of English. Niccola Muscia's two homoerotic sonnets were translated by Thomas Caldecott Chubb, who mistakenly interspersed them throughout Cecco Angiolieri's corpus; but Muscia's third sonnet, the insult of the poet Guido Cavalcanti, has not been translated. As part of Dante's complete oeuvre the *tenzone* with Forese Donati was translated by Kenelm Foster and Patrick Boyde. And Mino da Colle, Iacopo da Lèona, and Iacomo dei Tolomei have never been available at all to English readership. Of all the poets found in this volume only Dante is represented by a selection; the lyric productions of all the others are presented in their entirety.

This volume consists of a facing-page translation of the works, so that readers can refer to the originals; significant variations in the readings of the original texts are explained in footnotes. The language of Rustico and his imitators presents a unique challenge to the translator, as the English versions need to mirror the poet's stylistic flexibility. His amorous verse needs to read as love poetry. To that end, I have approximated the hendecasyllabic meter, but not the rhymes, of his sonnets; I have also used terminology suggestive of his higher lexicon. But his comic poetry is another matter altogether. It needs to reflect the aggressiveness — to 'pack the punch' — of his insults, and it needs to denote the offensive and sexual matters unflinchingly. Since he refers to many historical episodes and personages, each sonnet has a brief introductory comment, which explains some of the poet's references. It is important to bring Rustico's poetry to English readership. The praise / blame literary dichotomy is inherent to Dante's *Comedy* through its representations of the saintly in *Paradiso* and the damned in *Inferno*. As exemplified through Dante's *tenzone* with Forese Donati, Rustico is an important precursor to Dante, and essential to understanding Dante's masterpiece.

BIBLIOGRAPHY

I. English Translations

Angiolieri, Cecco, *The Sonnets of a Handsome and Well-Mannered Rogue*, trans., Thomas Caldecott Chubb (Hamden CT: Archon Books, 1970). Contains two sonnets by Niccola Muscia

Foster, Kenelm, and Patrick Boyde, *Dante's Lyric Poems* (Oxford: Clarendon Press, 1967). Contains the six sonnets of the *tenzone* between Dante and Forese Donati

Rossetti, Dante Gabriel, *Dante and His Circle with the Italian Poets Preceding Him (1100-1200-1300): A Collection of Lyrics* (Boston: Little Brown, 1905). Contains three sonnets by Rustico Filippi

Tusiani, Joseph, *The Age of Dante: An Anthology of Early Italian Poetry Translated into English Verse and with an Introduction* (New York: Baroque Press, 1974). Contains two sonnets by Rustico Filippi

II. Scholarly Editions

ALIGHIERI, DANTE, *Rime*, vol. 3, ed. by Domenico de Robertis (Florence: Le lettere, 2002), 451–60

BRUNI BETTARINI, ANNA, 'Le rime di Meo dei Tolomei e di Muscia da Siena', *Studi di filologia Italiana*, 33 (1974), 31–98.

DI FILIPPO, RUSTICO, *Sonetti*, ed. by Pier Vincenzo Mengaldo (Turin: Einaudi, 1971)

EGIDI, FRANCESCO, *Il libro di varie romanze volgare, cod. Vat. 3793* (Rome: Società filologica romana, 1902–1908). A diplomatic edition of the primary manuscript containing Rustico Filippi's poetry

FILIPPI, RUSTICO, *Sonetti amorosi e tenzone*, ed. by Silvia Buzzetti Gallarati (Rome: Carocci editore, 2009)

——, *Sonetti satirici e giocosi*, ed. by Silvia Buzzetti Gallarati (Rome: Carocci editore, 2005)

LINARDI, LINO, *I canzonieri della lirica italiana delle origini*, vol. 1, *Il canzoniere vaticano, Biblioteca Apostolica Vaticana Vat. Lat. 3793* (Florence: Edizioni del Galluzzo, 2000). A facsimile edition of the primary manuscript containing Rustico Filippi's poetry

MARRANI, GIUSEPPE, 'I sonetti di Rustico Filippi', *Studi di filologia italiana* 57 (1999), 33–196

MASSÉRA, ALDO FRANCESCO, ed., *Sonetti burleschi e realistici dei primi due secoli* (Bari: Laterza, 1940)

MARTI, MARIO, ed., *Poeti giocosi del tempo di Dante* (Milan: Rizzoli, 1956)

VITALE, MAURIZIO, ed., *Rimatori comico-realistici del Due e Trecento* (Turin: UTET, 1965)

III. Critical Studies: Rustico Filippi, Niccola Muscia, Mino da Colle, Iacopo da Lèona

ALFIE, FABIAN, 'Black Comedy: The Poetry of Niccola Muscia', *Romance Philology*, 61 (Fall 2007), 193–211

——, 'The Morality of Misogyny: The Case of Rustico Filippi, Vituperator of Women', *Quidditas*, 25 (2004), 43–70

——, 'Yes ... but was it funny? Cecco Angiolieri, Rustico Filippi, and Giovanni Boccaccio', in *Laughter in the Middle Ages and Early Modern Times: Epistemology of a Fundamental Human Behavior, its Meaning, and Consequences*, ed. by Albrecht Classen (Berlin, New York: De Gruyter, 2010), 265–82

APPLAUSO, NICOLINO, *Curses and Laughter: The Ethics of Political Invective in the Comic Poetry of High and Late Medieval Italy* (PhD Dissertation: University of Oregon, 2010)

——, 'Curses and Laughter in Medieval Italian Comic Poetry: The Ethics of Humor in Rustico Filippi's Invectives', in *Laughter in the Middle Ages and Early Modern Times: Epistemology of a Fundamental Human Behavior, its Meaning, and Consequences*, ed. by Albrecht Classen (Berlin, New York: De Gruyter, 2010), 383–412

APOLLONIO, MARIO, 'La realtà nuova e Folgore', in *Uomini e forme nella cultura italiana delle origini* (Florence: Sansoni, 1943), 282–301

BARTOLI, ADOLFO, 'La poesia giocosa e satirica in Toscana', in *Storia della letteratura italiana*, vol. 2 (Florence: Sansoni, 1879), 249–74

BISIACCO-HENRY, NELLA, 'L'invective dans la poésie comico-réaliste italienne', *Atalaya*, 5 (1994), 85–100

BUZZETTI GALLARATI, SILVIA, 'Alle origini di un linguaggio: la poesia satirica di Rustico Filippi (I)', *Medioevo romanzo*, 24 (2000), 346–84

——, 'Iacopo da Léona, "Segnori, udite strano malificio": Per una restituzione del senso', in *La parola al testo. Scritti per Bice Mortara Garavelli* (Alessandria: Edizioni dell'Orso, 2002), 745–62

——, 'La memoria di Rustico nel "Fiore"', in *Studi di filologia medievale offerti a D'Arco Silvio Avalle* (Milan-Naples: Ricciardi, 1996), 65–98

——, 'Onomastica equivoca nei sonetti sartirici di Rustico Filippi', in *Cecco Angiolieri e la poesia satirica medievale. Atti del convegno internazionale Siena, 26-27 ottobre 2002*, ed. by Stefano Carrai and Giuseppe Marrani (Florence: Edizioni del Galluzzo, 2005), 51–75

——, 'Rustico "comico" in Va. (ms. Vaticano Latino 4823)', *Rivista di studi testuali*, 3 (2001), 63–95

——, 'Rustico "cortese" in Va. (ms. Vaticano Latino 4823)', *Rivista di studi testuali*, 4 (2002), 77–103

——, 'Sull'organizzazione del discorso comico nella produzione giocosa di Rustico Filippi', *Medioevo romanzo*, 9.2 (August 1984), 189–213

CASINI, TOMMASO, 'Un poeta umorista del secolo XIII', in *Studi danteschi* (Città del Castello: Lapi, 1913), 225–55

CIAN, VITTORIO, *La satira* (Milan: Vallardi, 1929), 135–38

DA BARBERINO, FRANCESCO, *I documenti d'amore*, vol. 1, ed. by Francesco Egidi (Milan: Archè, 1982), 88–101

FEDERICI, VINCENZO, *Le rime di Rustico di Filippo rimatore fiorentino del sec. XIII* (Bergamo: Arti Grafiche, 1889)
FOLENA, GIANFRANCO, 'Cultura poetica dei primi fiorentini', *Giornale storico della letteratura italiana*, 147: 457 (1970), 1–42
GIUNTA, CLAUDIO, 'Un'ipotesi sulla morfologia del canzoniere Vaticano Lat. 3793', *Studi di filologia italiana*, 53 (1995), 23–54
GUERRIERI-CROCETTI, CAMILLO, *La lirica predantesca* (Florence: Vallecchi, 1925)
LATINI, BRUNETTO, 'Il Favolello', in *Il Tesoretto e il Favolello* (Strasburg: J. H. Ed. Heitz, 1900), 98–102
LEVIN, JOAN H., *Rustico di Filippo and the Florentine Lyric Tradition* (New York: Peter Lang, 1986)
MANCA, FRANCO, 'Dante e la poesia realistico-borghese', *Canadian Journal of Italian Studies*, 8.30 (1985), 32–45
MARTI, MARIO, *Cecco Angiolieri e i poeti autobiografici tra il 200 e il 300* (Lecce: Galatina, 1945–1946)
——, 'La coscienza stilistica di Rustico di Filippo e la sua poesia', in *Cultura e stile nei poeti giocosi del tempo di Dante* (Pisa: Nistri-Lischi, 1953), 41–58
——, 'Revisione ed interpretazione di due sonetti di Rustico di Filippo', *Giornale storico della letteratura italiana*, 129 (1952), 26–30
MENESCALCHI, ROMANO, 'Osservazioni sulla "lonza" in Rustico Filippi e Dante', *Studi danteschi*, 74 (2009), 127–47
MENGALDO, PIER VINCENZO, 'Un "vicino" di Dante: Rustico Filippo', in *Linguistica e retorica di Dante* (Pisa: Nistri-Lischi, 1978), 247–60
MONGIAT, CATERINA, 'Realismo e pluralità di stili nei ritratti femminili di Rustico di Filippo', in *Studi in onore di Pier Vincenzo Mengaldo per i suoi settant'anni* (Firenze: Tavernuzze, 2007), 221–36
ORVIETO, PAOLO, and BRESTOLINI, LUCIA, *La poesia comico-realistica: dalle origini al Cinquecento* (Rome: Carocci, 2000)
PERCOPO, ERASMO, 'Il *Fiore* è di Rustico di Filippo?', *Rassegna critica della letteratura italiana*, 11 (1906), 49–59
PERRUS, CLAUDE, 'L'invective politique dans l'Italie du Moyen Age', *Atalaya*, 5 (1994), 179–92
PETROCCHI, GIORGIO, 'I poeti realisti', in *Le origini e il Duecento*, vol. 1: *Storia della letteratura italiana*, eds. Emilio Cecchi and Natalino Sapegno (Milan: Garzanti, 1965), 689–725
PREVITERA, CARMELO, 'Poeti burleschi e realistici dei secoli XIII e XIV', in *La poesia giocosa e l'umorismo* (Milan: Vallardi, 1939), 143–84
REIM, RICCARDO, 'Eros, il demone', in *Il corpo della Musa: Erotismo e pornografia nella letteratura dal '200 al '900. Storia / Antologia / Dizionario* (Rome: Riuniti, 2002), vii–lxvii
ROSSI, LUCIANO, 'I sonetti di Jacopo da Leona', in *Il genere 'tenzone' nelle letterature romanze delle Origini*, ed. by Matteo Pedroni and Antonio Stäuble (Ravenna: Longo Editore, 1999), 111–3.
RUSSO, VITTORIO, '"Verba obscena" e comico: Rustico Filippi', *Filologia e critica*, 5.2–3 (maggio–dicembre, 1980), 169–82
SAIBER, ARIELLE, 'Rustico di Filippo', in *Enciclopedia of Italian Literary Studies*,

vol. 2, ed. by Gaetana Marrone and Paolo Puppa (New York: Routledge, 2007), 1635–37

SANTANGELO, SALVATORE, *Le tenzoni poetiche nella letteratura italiana* (Geneva: Olschki, 1928), 39–41

EUGENIO SAVONA, 'Rustico di Filippo e la poesia comico-realistica', in *Cultura e ideologia nell'età comunale. Ricerche sulla letteratura italiana dell'età comunale* (Ravenna: Longo Editore, 1975), 57–70

SUITNER, FRANCO, *La poesia satirica e giocosa nell'età dei comuni* (Padua: Antenore, 1983)

TROUSSELARD, SYLVAIN, 'Le *Vituperium* comme forme inversée de la *Lauda* chez Cenne da La Chitarra d'Arezzo et Rustico Filippi', in *L'Invective: Histoire, Formes, Stratégies: Actes du Colloque Internationale des 24 et 25 Novembre 2005, Saint-Etienne* (Saint-Etienne: Universitè de Saint-Etienne, 2006), 21–36

VITALE, MAURIZIO, *La lingua dei poeti realistico-giocosi del '200 e del '300* (Milan: La Goliardica, 1955)

WIERUSZOWSKI, HELENE, '"Ars dictaminis" in the Time of Dante', in *Politics and Culture in Medieval Spain and Italy* (Rome: Edizioni di storia e letteratura, 1971), 359–86

——, 'Mino da Colle di Val d'Elsa: Rimatore e dettatore al tempo di Dante', in *Politics and Culture in Medieval Spain and Italy* (Rome: Edizioni di storia e letteratura, 1971), 347–57.

IV. Critical Studies: Dante's *Tenzone* with Forese Donati

ALFIE, FABIAN, *Dante's* Tenzone *with Forese Donati: The Reprehension of Vice* (Toronto: University of Toronto Press, 2011)

——, 'For Want of a Nail: The Guerri-Lanza-Cursietti Argument about the *Tenzone*', *Dante Studies*, 116 (1998), 141–59

——, 'Rustico's Reputation: Ramifications for Dante's *Tenzone* with Forese Donati', *Electronic Bulletin of the Dante Society of America* (*EBDSA*): <http://www.princeton.edu/~dante/ebdsa/index.html> (linked under 'Minor Works')

BARBI, MICHELE, 'Ancora della tenzone di Dante con Forese', *Studi danteschi*, 16 (1932), 69–103

——, 'Tenzone con Forese Donati', in *Rime della 'Vita Nuova' e della giovinezza*, vol. 2: *Opere di Dante*, ed. by Michele Barbi and F. Maggini (Florence: Le Monnier, 1956), 279–373

——, 'La tenzone di Dante con Forese Donati', *Studi danteschi*, 9 (1924), 5–149

BARTLETT, ELIZABETH and ILLIANO, ANTONIO, 'Dante's Tenzone', *Italica*, 44 (1967), 282–90

——, 'The Young Dante: Opposing Views', *Italian Quarterly*, 10.38 (1966), 57–67

BORRIERO, GIOVANNI, 'Considerazioni sulla tradizione manoscritta della *Tenzone* di Dante con Forese', in *Antico Moderno*, vol. 4: *I numeri* (Rome: Bagatto Libri, 1997), 385–405

BOSCO, UMBERTO, 'Forese', in *Dante vicino* (Rome: Caltanissetta, 1985), 150–71

CARDUCCI, GIOSUÈ, 'Delle rime di Dante', in *Prose di Giosuè Carducci. MDCCCLIX–MCMIII* (Bologna: Zanichelli, 1922), 27–143

CHERCHI, PAOLO, 'Pentangulo, Nodo di Salomone, Pentacolo', *Lingua Nostra*, 39.2–3 (giugno–settembre 1978), 33–36

CHIARINI, EUGENIO, 'Ben so che fosti figliuol d'Alighieri', in *Enciclopedia dantesca*, vol. 1 (Rome: Istituto della Enciclopedia Italiana, 1970), 590

——, 'Ben ti faranno il nodo Salamone', in *Enciclopedia dantesca*, vol. 1 (Rome: Istituto della Enciclopedia Italiana, 1970), 591

——, 'Bicci novel, figliuol di non so cui', in *Enciclopedia dantesca*, vol. 1 (Rome: Istituto della Enciclopedia Italiana, 1970), 630–31

——, 'Chi udisse tossir la malfatata', in *Enciclopedia dantesca*, vol. 1 (Rome: Istituto della Enciclopedia Italiana, 1970), 979–80

——, 'L'altra notte mi venne una gran tosse', in *Enciclopedia dantesca*, vol. 3 (Rome: Istituto della Enciclopedia Italiana, 1971), 555

——, 'Tenzone', in *Enciclopedia dantesca*, vol. 5 (Rome: Istituto della Enciclopedia Italiana, 1976), 561–63

——, 'Va, rivesti San Gal prima che dichi', in *Enciclopedia dantesca*, vol. 5 (Rome: Istituto della Enciclopedia Italiana, 1970), 887

CONTINI, GIANFRANCO, 'Filologia ed esegesi dantesca', in *Un'idea di Dante. Saggi danteschi* (Torino: Einaudi, 2001), 113–42

CUDINI, PIERO, 'La tenzone tra Dante e Forese e la "Commedia" (Inf. XXX; Purg. XXIII–XXIV)', *Giornale storico della letteratura italiana*, 158 (1982), 1–25

CURSIETTI, MAURO, 'Dante e Forese alla taverna del Panìco. Le prove documentarie della falsità della tenzone', *L'Alighieri*, 16.41 (luglio–dicembre 2000), 8–22

——, 'I doppi sensi del sonetto "S'e' non ti caggia la tua santalena"', *La parola del testo: semestrale di filologia e letteratura italiana e comparata dal medioevo al rinascimento*, 3 (1999), 75–83

——, *La falsa tenzone di Dante con Forese Donati* (Rome: De Rubeis, 1995)

——, 'Motti e facezie da Rustico Filippi al Burchiello', *La parola del testo: semestrale di filologia e letteratura italiana e comparata dal medioevo al rinascimento*, 7 (2003), 63–90

——, 'Nuovi contributi per l'apocrifia della cosiddetta *tenzone di Dante con Forese Donati* ovvero *la tenzone del Panìco*', in *Bibliografia e critica dantesca: Saggi dedicati a Enzo Esposito*, ed. by V. De Gregorio (Ravenna: Longo, 1997), 53–72

——, 'Una beffa parallela alla falsa *Tenzone di Dante con Forese Donati*: la berta di Cavalcanti "cavalcato"', *L'Alighieri*, 13.40 (gennaio–giugno 1999), 91–110

CHIAPPELLI, FREDI, 'Proposta d'interpretazione per la tenzone di Dante con Forese Donati', *Giornale storico della letteratura italiana*, 142 (1966), 321–50

DEL LUNGO, ISIDORO, 'La tenzone di Dante con Forese Donati', in *Dante ne' tempi di Dante* (Bologna: Zanichelli, 1888), 435–61

DEL MONTE, ALBERTO, 'Forese', *Cultura e scuola*, 4.13–14 (1965), 572–89

DE ROBERTIS, DOMENICO, 'Ancora per Dante e Forese Donati', in *'Feconde venner le carte'. Studi in onore di Ottavio Besomi*, ed. by T. Crivelli (Bellinzona: Casagrande, 1997), 35–48

DÍAZ, SARA E., 'Contested Virilities: Constructing Masculinity in Dante's *Tenzone* with Forese', *Italian Culture*, 32.1 (March 2014), 1–19

FILIPPINI, FRANCESCO, 'Il "nodo di Salomone" nella tenzone di Dante e Forese', *Il giornale dantesco* 25.1 (gennaio–marzo 1922), 237–42

GIUFFREDA, TOMMASO, *Dante e Forese* (Bari: Danisi, 1952)

GUIBERTEAU, PHILIPPE, 'La "Tenzone" ou "dispute avec Forese Donati"', *Bulletin de l'Association Guillaume Bude*, 1.1 (1970), 169–184

GUERRI, DOMENICO, 'Ancora il "gagno" d'Alighero', in *Scritti danteschi e d'altra letteratura antica*, ed. by Antonio Lanza (Rome: De Rubeis, 1990), 339–54

——, *La corrente popolare nel rinascimento: Berte burle e baie nella Firenze del Brunellesco e del Burchiello* (Florence: Sansoni, 1931)

——, 'Elementi del *Decamerone* nel primo sonetto d' "Alighiero" con Bicci', in *Scritti danteschi e d'altra letteratura antica*, ed., Antonio Lanza (Rome: De Rubeis, 1990), 367–78

——, 'Per la storia di Monna Tessa', in *Scritti danteschi e d'altra letteratura antica*, ed. by Antonio Lanza (Rome: De Rubeis, 1990), 355–65

JENNI, ADOLFO, 'Donati, Forese', in *Enciclopedia dantesca*, vol. 2 (Rome: Istituto della Enciclopedia Italiana, 1970), 560–63

LANZA, ANTONIO, 'A norma di filologia: ancora a proposito della cosiddetta "Tenzone tra Dante e Forese"', *L'Alighieri*, 10.38 (luglio–dicembre, 1997), 43–54

——, 'Una volgare lite nella Firenze del primo quattrocento: la cosiddetta tenzone di Dante con Forese Donati — nuovi contributi alla tesi di Domenico Guerri', in *Polemiche e berte letterarie nella Firenze del primo quattrocento* (Rome: Bulzoni, 1971), 396–409

MANCA, FRANCO, 'Dante e la poesia realistico-borghese', *Canadian Journal of Italian Studies*, 8.30 (1985), 32–45

MANGIERI, CONO, 'Gentucca Dantesca e dintorni', *Italian Quarterly*, 32.125–26 (Summer–Fall 1995), 5–25

——, 'Gentucca ... figlia spuria di Dante?', Giuseppe Bonghi: Progetto Dante Alighieri website: <http://www.fausernet.novara.it/fauser/biblio/index042.htm>

MARTI, MARIO, 'Sulla genesi del realismo dantesco', in *Realismo dantesco e altri studi* (Milan-Naples: Ricciardi, 1961), 1–32

——, 'Verso il "realismo": la tenzone e le pietrose', in *Dante, Boccaccio, Leopardi* (Naples: Liguori, 1980), 13–35

MOMIGLIANO, ATTILIO, 'Un apocrifo di Dante?', in *Elzeviri* (Florence: Felice Le Monnier, 1945), 39–44

NOAKES, SUSAN, 'Virility, Nobility, and Banking: The Crossing of Discourses in the *Tenzone* with Forese', in *Dante for the New Millennium*, ed. by Teodolinda Barolini and H. Wayne Storey (New York: Fordham University Press, 2003), 241–51

PREVITERA, CARMELO, 'Nell'età del Rinascimento', in *La poesia giocosa e l'umorismo dalle origini al Rinascimento* (Milan: Vallardi, 1939), 237–307

QUAGLIO, ENZO ANTONIO, 'Intorno alla tenzone Dante-Forese', in *'Per correr miglior acque ...' Bilanci e prospettive degli studi danteschi alle soglie del nuovo millennio. Atti del Convegno internazionale di Verona-Ravenna, 25–29 ottobre 1999*, vol. 1 (Rome: Salerno, 2001), 247–80

SANSONI, UMBERTO, *Il nodo di Salomone. Simbolo e archetipo d'alleanza* (Milan: Electa, 1998)

SAVARESE, GENNARO, 'Una proposta per Forese: Dante e il "memorar presente"', *Rassegna della letteratura italiana*, 94 (1990), 5–20

SENO REED, COSETTA, '"A guisa d'un nodo di Salomone": *I Promessi Sposi*, XV', *Rassegna Europea della Letteratura Italiana*, 23 (2004), 111–15

SIMONCINI, DANIELE, 'Dante e Forese: storia di un autoschediasma', *L'Alighieri*, 8.36 (1995), 67–74

STÄUBLE, ANTONIO, 'La tenzone di Dante con Forese Donati', *Letture classensi*, 24 (1995), 151–70

STEFANINI, RUGGERO, 'Tenzone sì e tenzone no', *Lectura Dantis*, 18–19 (Spring–Fall 1996), 111–28

WITTE, CARLO [KARL], 'Rime in testi antichi attribuite a Dante', in *Tre Articoli* (Lipsia: Brockhaus, 1871), 257–302

ZACCARELLO, MICHELANGELO, 'L'uovo o la gallina? *Purg.* XXIII e la tenzone di Dante e Forese Donati', *L'Alighieri*, 22 (2003), 5–26

RUSTICO FILIPPI

1.[1] A voi, messere Iacopo comare,
Rustico s'acomanda fedelmente,
e dice, se vendetta avete a fare,
ch'e' la farà di buon cuor lëalmente.

Ma piaceriagli forte che 'l parlare
e·rider vostro fosse men sovente,
ché male perdere uom, che guadagnare,
suole schifare più la mala gente.

E forte si crucciò[2] di monna Nese
quando sonetto udì di lei novello;
e credel dimostrar tosto in palese.

Ma troppo siete conto di Fastello,
fino a tanto ch'egli ha danar da spese:
ond'e' si crede bene esser donzello.

[1] Rustico's poetry is cited from Rustico Di Filippo, *Sonetti*, ed., Pier Vincenzo Mengaldo (Turin: Einaudi, 1971). Variants are taken from the following editions: Rustico Filippi, *Sonetti amorosi e tenzone*, ed., Silvia Buzzetti Gallarati (Rome: Carocci editore, 2009) for sonnets 1–28; Rustico Filippi, *Sonetti satirici e giocosi*, ed., Silvia Buzzetti Gallarati (Rome: Carocci editore, 2005), for sonnets 30-59; Aldo Francesco Masséra, ed., *Sonetti burleschi e realistici dei primi due secoli* (Bari: Laterza, 1940); Mario Marti, ed., *Poeti giocosi del tempo di Dante* (Milan: Rizzoli, 1956); Maurizio Vitale, ed., *Rimatori comico-realistici del Due e Trecento* (Turin: UTET, 1965).
[2] Masséra: 'cruccia'.

Sonnets 1–2: Deal with Fastello di Attaviano de' Tosinghi, a Guelph who in 1259 was *podestà* of San Gimignano.

1. This sonnet is addressed to messer Iacopo, possibly Iacopo Rusticucci (*Inferno* 16), or Iacopo di messer Attaviano dell'Acerbo. If the former, then he was a Ghibelline; if the latter, then he was the father of Acerbo and Cambio of sonnets 6–8. It is not clear who lady Nese is. Dante speaks with Iacopo Rusticucci in canto 16 of *Inferno* among the sodomites, and Rusticucci complains of his 'fierce wife' (v. 45); if Filippi is writing about the same individual, then his apostrophe of him as 'godmother' would appear to be a slur on his sexuality.

> To you, messer Iacopo godmother,
> Rustico faithfully commends himself
> and he says, if you need to seek vengeance,
> he'll do so loyally and with a good heart.
>
> But he would prefer it if your speech
> and laughter took place less frequently;
> whoever wants to avoid evil or to earn
> usually avoids above all evil people.
>
> He got quite angry with lady Nese
> when he heard the new sonnet about her
> and he thinks it spelled out too much about her.
>
> But you are too much Fastello's friend,
> at least as long as he has money to spend:
> for he rightly thinks he's a young gentleman.

2. Fastel, messer fastidio de la cazza
dibassa i ghebellini a dismisura,
e tutto il giorno aringa in su la piazza
e dice ch'e' gli tiene 'n aventura.

E chi 'l contende, nel viso gli sprazza
velen, che v'è mischiato altra sozzura,
e sì la notte come 'l dì schiamazza.
Or Dio ci menovasse la sciagiura![1]

Ond'io 'l ti fo saper, dinanzi assai
ch'a man vegni de' tuo' nemici guelfi,
s'è temp'è se vendetta non ne fai.

Ma tu n'avrai merzé, quando il vedrai.
Fammi cotanto: togligli Montelfi,
così di duol morir tosto il vedrai.

---

[1] Massèra renders this line as direct discourse.

2. About the feigned bravery of Fastello di Attaviano de' Tosinghi, a Guelph, who had taken control of the castle Montelfi in the Arno valley.

>Fastello, messer ball-breaker[1]
>tears down the Ghibellines beyond all measure,
>and harangues them all day long in the piazza
>and says that he considers them all to be in danger.
>
>Whoever challenges him sprays poison
>in his face, which is mixed with other filth,
>and he makes such a din, whether night or day.
>May God now spare us from this shame!
>
>So I'll have you know, before too long
>you'll fall into the Guelphs' enemy hands,
>since for so long you haven't sought a vendetta.
>
>But you'll take pity on him when you see him.
>Do this much for me: take away Montelfi
>from him so you can watch him die in pain.

---

[1] Literally, 'penis irritation'.

3. A voi, che ve ne andaste per paura:
sicuramente potete tornare;
da ch'e' ci è dirizzata la ventura,
ormai potete guerra inconinzare.

E' più non vi bisogna stare a dura,
da che nonn-è chi vi scomunicare:
ma ben lo vi tenete 'n isciagura
che non avete più cagion che dare.

Ma so bene, se Carlo fosse morto,
che voi ci trovereste ancor cagione;
però del papa nonn-ho gran conforto.

Ma io non voglio con voi stare a tenzone,
ca·llungo temp'è ch'io ne fui accorto
che 'l ghibellino aveste per garzone.

3. A sonnet decrying the cowardice of fellow Ghibellines, who fled after the battle of Benevento in 1266, when the Guelphs, led by Charles I of Anjou, were victorious. In this sonnet Rustico also refers to the papal use of excommunication to achieve political ends.

> To you, who all ran off out of fear:
> you can securely return home now.
> Since bad fortune has turned against us
> you can now begin to wage war.
>
> No longer should you be on the defensive
> since there's no one to excommunicate you.
> But still you should consider it a pity
> that you provide them no cause to do so.
>
> But I know well that if Charles had died
> you would find ample reasons for it;
> but I take little comfort from the Pope.
>
> But I don't want to stand and argue,
> for it's been so long since I found out
> that you thought of the Ghibellines as servants.

4. Su, donna Gemma, co·lla farinata
e col buon vino e co·l'uova ricenti
che la Mita per voi sia argomentata,
ch'io veggio ben ch'ell'ha alegati i denti.

Non vedete com'ell'è sottigliata?
Maravigliar ne fate tutte genti.
Donna Filippa assai n'è biasimata
da tutti i suoi amici e parenti.

Or accendete il foco e sì cocete
cosa che spesso in bocca si metta;[1]
se non, per certo morir la farete:

ché la gonella, che sì l'era stretta,
se ne porian far due, be·llo vedete,
così è fatta magra e sotiletta.

---

[1] Massèra: 'la si metta'.

Sonnets 4–5: About Gemma, Filippa and Mita. Almost nothing is known about these women. One document notes that two poor women, Gemma and Filippa, lived together in 1305 in a house owned by Lippo Aldobrandeschi. These sonnets deal with Mita's sudden thinness (perhaps due to an abortion?).

4.   Come on, lady Gemma, with the mush
    and with the good wine, and with the fresh eggs —
    for Mita has been purging herself
    and I can see she's wired her mouth shut.

    Don't you see how skinny she's gotten?
    You're making everyone marvel.
    Lady Filippa's already been blamed
    by all of her friends and relatives.

    Light the fire right away and cook something
    that she can put in her mouth straight away;
    if you don't, surely you'll watch her die.

    Because her skirt, which used to be so tight
    is now enough for two — surely you see it! —
    for now she's so skinny and bony.

5. Se no l'atate, fate villania,
    però ch'io dubbio non sia intisichita:
    di belle tortellette le faria,
    ché vedete che nonn-ha de la vita.

    Oi lasso me, com'ell'è gita via!
    Per Dio, pensate come sia guerita,
    ché, non ch'a voi, a me ne 'ncresceria:
    più rangola dovreste aver di Mita.

    E spïate qual fosse la cagione
    ond'ell'ha sì perduto il manicare,
    che si suole sì atar per ficazone;

    e quando fosse sopra al vendemmiare,
    non si tenea le man sotto il gherone:
    ed or s'è sì lasciata dimagrare.

5. If you don't help her, you commit villainy,
because I fear that she's tuberculous;
you should make her some nice little cakes
because you can see that she has no life left.

Oh poor me, how she's wasted away!
By God, think about how she can be cured
because I'd regret it — wouldn't you?
You should pay more attention to Mita

and figure out what might be the cause
that she has so lost her appetite
you can help her only by force-feeding her.

And how was it that at the last harvest
she couldn't fit her hand under her belt
and now she's let herself get so skinny?

6. Volete udir vendetta smisurata
c'ha·fatta di sua donna l'Acerbuzzo?
La barba lunga un mese n'ha portata
orando che dovea far Giovannuzzo.

Dio, com' bene le stette a la sciaurata,
quand'ella soferia così gran puzzo!
Per quella via ne va da·la cognata,
s'altra vendetta nonn-è di Cambiuzzo.

Dunque, ben n'anderà per quella via:
che 'nmantenente fue passato il duolo
ch'e la dissotterrò, perché putia.

Almen faccia vendetta del figliolo!
Ma per quel ch'io spero che ne sia,
per un fiorin voglio esser cavigliuolo.

Sonnets 6–8: Three sonnets about Acerbo and Cambio, who were the sons of messer Attaviano dell'Acerbo. In 1268, they were banished along with their father and another brother, Neri, as Ghibellines.

6. This enigmatic sonnet appears to deal with Acerbo's return to Florence, when he discovered that his wife had given birth to an illegitimate child. Most scholars interpret it as criticizing his weak punishment of her for her adultery; Filippi often depicts sexually misbehaving women as smelly. Instead of enforcing his rights as a husband, Filippi suggests, Acerbo wandered the streets and grew a long beard, like the mendicant friar Giovannuzzo. But exactly why Acerbo takes the road to his sister-in-law's house isn't clear, nor is the final verse.

> Do you want to hear the outrageous vendetta
> that Acerbuzzo brought down upon his wife?
> For a month he went about with a long beard
> praying much like Giovannuzzo did.
>
> God! How much she deserved it, the wretch,
> when she would suffer such a great stench!
> He takes the road to his sister-in-law's house,
> since there's no other pay-back for Cambiuzzo.
>
> Therefore, he would do well to go down that road:
> but as soon as his pain was over
> he dug her up, because she smelled badly.
>
> He should at least avenge himself for the son!
> But, from what I expect will happen,
> I would give a florin to be a peg.

7. No riconoscereste voi l'Acerbo,
ancor che voi il vedeste molto a sera?
Sì fareste, ch'e' non fue da Viterbo
nonn-è ancora una semana intera.

Del compagno nol dico, che 'l mi serbo,
ché troppo arosserebbe ne la cera;
in pasto il tegno e tuttavia lo 'nerbo,
ché v'era or con via maggiore schiera.

Non ch'io v'aprisse, monna lëonessa!
Sì gra·lezzo vi vien per la quintana
ch'altri avrà quella peverada spessa.

Molto vi mostravate piemontana:
fatta siete reina, di contessa:
Frian v'aspetta quest'altra semana.

7. Also about Acerbo and Cambio, who apparently returned from exile in Viterbo, a stronghold of the Guelphs. Rustico derides a woman, Lady Lioness, for her adultery by describing her stench (see sonnet 20, where he talks about lions as smelly); he refers to her unclean genitals as an odorous 'peppered stew' and as a quintain, the target for jousting-practice. She seems to have used sex as a means to climb socially like a woman of the Piedmont, transforming from a countess to the queen of the San Frediano (Frian) neighborhood.

> Wouldn't you recognize Acerbo
> although you saw him well into the evening?
> Surely so, for he is back from Viterbo;
> it's now been less than a complete week.
>
> I don't speak of your friend — I'll wait till later —
> because he would become too red-faced;
> I will pummel him and strike him soon,
> because he had with him a stronger group.
>
> Not that I pried you open, Lady Lioness!
> For a great stench came from your quintain,
> but other men will have that thick peppered stew.
>
> And you showed yourself to be so Piedmontese
> that, from a countess, you've become a queen,
> and Frian awaits you in another week.

8. Due donzei nuovi ha oggi in questa terra
c'hanno sì vinti ciascun fiorentino
che più non possor sofrire la guerra:
l'un è l'Acerbo e l'altro è Guadagnino.

Questi due ci hanno messi a sì gran serra
che ne ripiace molto Bonfantino:
e quinci si racorga, s'alcun ci erra,
che macine non son già di molino:

ch'elle non hanno fondo, ma stranezza
hanno di peso, sì che lo palmento
n'andria giù in perfondo per gravezza,

ché di piombo è ciascun lor reggimento.
Chi gli bestemmia, molto abbia alegrezza,
e chi non, sì gli basti esto tormento.

8. In addition to featuring Acerbo, this sonnet refers to two other individuals, Guadagnino and Bonfantino. The former is probably Guadagnino, son of Gottifredo, who took part in the battle of Montaperti on the side of the Ghibellines. The latter may be Bonfantino Mascheroni, who in 1269 was among the Ghibellines of the San Pancrazio neighborhood. In this sonnet Rustico appears to criticize them for their obesity.

> There are two new pageboys in this land
> who've defeated every other Florentine
> who can't endure the war any longer:
> one's Acerbo, the other's Guadagnino.
>
> Those two men have us so cornered
> that we like and re-like Bonfantino;
> and he should see, if we aren't wrong,
> that these grindstones don't belong in mills.
>
> Because these stones lack foundations, but strangeness
> they have in pounds, such that the floor
> could give way below them thanks to their weight
>
> since lead is their every support.
> Whoever curses them should feel great joy,
> and for who doesn't may this pain suffice.

9.   Collui che puose nome al Macinella
    al mio parer non fue strolago fino,
    ché — dico questo a voi non per novella —
    ch'egli 'l dovea serbar per ser Laino.

    Ché qual cavallo il porta in su la sella
    non vuole esser puledro nè ronzino:
    ch'e' vela gli occhi e sì grale[1] favella
    che 'l mar passo per esser saracino!

    Ched egli avanza e passa ogn'altro grave
    che fosse o sia o possa essere al mondo,
    e di·cciò porta ben seco la chiave.

    Ed haccene un, che non ha il capo biondo,
    che 'n mar vorria che fosse co·llui i·nave,
    perch'ambendue n'andassero in profondo.

---

[1] Massèra: 'grave'.

9. It is unclear who Macinella and ser Laino are. The former may be Macinella de' Quercetani, who lived in the neighborhood of San Miniato al Monte in 1288. Rustico puns on Macinella's nickname ('millstone'), stressing ser Laino's obesity instead. It may also be that the grindstones of the previous sonnet ('macine', v. 8) are an allusion to him.

>
> Whoever named him Macinella
> wasn't a keen astrologer it seems,
> because — I tell you this as no great news —
> he should have saved the name for Ser Laino:
>
> whichever horse bears him in its saddle
> shouldn't be a colt or an old nag:
> its eyes cloud over and it feebly whimpers
> as he crossed[1] the sea to be a Saracen.
>
> Since he exceeds any other heavy weight
> which is or was or could be in the world,
> and he alone holds the key to heaviness.
>
> And there is one man (without a blond head)
> whom I would want with him in a ship at sea
> because both would go straight down to the depths.

---

[1] Early editors (e.g., Federici, D'Ancona) read this as a past tense: 'as he crossed'. That reading seems to reflect better the manuscript.

10. Messer Bertuccio, a dritto uom vi cagiona
che Fazio non guardate del veleno,
e ciascun fiorentin di ciò ragiona,
ch'e' non va ben sicuro a pallafreno.

Un gran distrier di pregio hae a Chermona,
che mille livre il dice in tutto 'l meno:
fate che vegna per la sua persona;
non siate scarso in sua guardia, nè leno.

E questo dico, e vo' che sia[1] sentenza
credendo il me' di voi dicer, per vero:
messer Bertuccio il guardi per Fiorenza,

che de lo 'ngegno suo sta cavaliero;
e 'l Chiocciolo gli deggia far credenza.
Non ch'io ne dotti, tant'ha il viso fiero.

---

[1] Buzzetti Gallarati: 'si' a'.

10. A sonnet about messer Bertuccio, or Lambertuccio di messer Ghino Frescobaldi, Fazio the notary, and Lambertuccio's brother, Giovanni, nicknamed Chiocciolo ('snail'). Bertuccio is supposed to defend Fazio, but Fazio's weakness is evident to everyone.

>Messer Bertuccio, everyone rightly accuses
>you for not preventing slander of Fazio,
>and every Florentine talks about how
>he doesn't ride securely on his palfrey.
>
>There's a great worthy charger in Cremona
>which he says is worth at least a thousand *lire*;
>have it come to take care of his needs —
>don't be cheap nor lacking as his guard.
>
>I say this, and I want it to be true
>believing that I speak the best for you, in faith:
>Bertuccio should watch over him through Florence,
>
>because his wisdom will make a knight of him,
>and Chiocciolo needs to believe it.
>Not that I doubt it — his face is so fierce.

11. Oi dolce mio marito Aldobrandino,
rimanda ormai il farso suo a Pilletto,
ch'egli è tanto cortese fante e fino
che creder non déi ciò che te n'è detto.

E no star tra la gente a capo chino,
ché non se' bozza, e fòtine disdetto;
ma sì come amorevole vicino
co·noi venne a dormir nel nostro letto.

Rimanda il farso ormai, più no il tenere,
ch'e' mai non ci verrà oltre tua voglia,
poi che n'ha conosciuto il tuo volere.

Nel nostro letto già mai non si spoglia.
Tu non dovéi gridare, anzi tacere:
ch'a me non fece cosa ond'io mi doglia.

11. It is not clear who Aldobrandino, his wife, or Pilletto were. This sonnet, written in the wife's voice, attempts to exonerate Pilletto for having left a doublet — a type of undershirt — in their bedroom. After all, she stresses, nothing he did caused her any pain (thus he might have given her pleasure instead).

>Oh my sweet husband Aldobrandino,
>return the doublet back to Pilletto.
>He's such a fine and a courtly young lad
>that you shouldn't believe what you've been told.
>
>And don't go through the crowd hanging your head —
>you're not a cuckold and I can prove it.
>But like a sweet and loving neighbor
>he came to sleep with us in our bed.
>
>Send back his doublet now, don't keep it anymore,
>and he won't come again against your wishes
>now that he knows exactly what you want.
>
>He never gets undressed in our bed.
>You shouldn't have yelled — you should keep quiet! —
>since he did nothing that I could complain of.

12. D'una diversa cosa ch'è aparita
consiglio ch'abbian guardia i fiorentini;
e qual è quei che vuol campar la vita,
sì mandi al Veglio per suoi asessini.

Ché ci ha una lonza sì fera ed ardita
che, se Carlo sapesse i suo' confini
e de la sua prodezza avesse udita,
tosto n'andrebbe sopra i Saracini.

Ma chi è questa lonza or lo sacciate:
Paniccia egli è. Che fate, o da Fiorenza,
ch'oste no stanzïate o cavalcate?

Che s'e' seguisce inanzi sua valenza
com'egli ha fatta adietro, sì gli date
sicuramente in guardia la Proenza.

12. A mock warning to Charles I of Anjou, King of Naples, about his threats to Florence. The king should employ the legendary Old Man of the Mountain, who controlled the assassins, because Paniccia Frescobaldi is as fierce as a leopard, Rustico asserts. Rustico is probably writing ironically, emphasizing Paniccia's actual ineffectiveness in battle. In sonnet 24 Rustico again alludes to the legend of the Old Man of the Mountain, the leader of the Assassins.

The sonnet was probably written in the 1280s because in that decade the Florentine government possessed a live leopard as a symbol of its power; and Charles I of Anjou died in 1285.

Because of a strange thing that's appeared
I suggest that the Florentines stay on guard,
and whoever wants to remain alive
should send to the Old Man for his assassins;

because there's a leopard so fierce and brave
that if Charles knew the boundaries,
and if he knew about its courage,
he'd sooner take on the Saracens.

But now you should know who this leopard is:
Paniccia. Now, what will you Florentines do
since you don't stop the enemy or charge?

Because if he showed his valor in advancing
as much as in retreat, you would put
Provence securely under his protection.

13. Una bestiola ho vista molto fera,
armata forte d'una nuova guerra,
a cui risiede sì la cervelliera
che de·legnaggio par di Salinguerra.

Se 'nsino 'l mento avesse la gorgiera,
conquisterebbe il mar, non che la terra;
e chi paventa e dotta sua visera
al mio parer nonn-è folle ned erra.

Laid'ha la cera e periglioso ha 'l piglio,
e burfa spesso a guisa di leone:
torrebbe 'l tinto a cui desse di piglio;

e gli occhi ardenti ha via più che leone:
de' suoi nemici asai mi maraviglio
sed e' non muoion sol di pensagione.

13. It is unknown who this 'fierce warrior' is. However, almost certainly Rustico is being ironic, underscoring the man's actual cowardice. In the process, Rustico contrasts him to the members of the Salinguerra, a powerful Ghibelline family from Ferrara.

> I saw a most ferocious beast
> strongly armed with new weapons
> and whose helmet fits so well —
> he seems to be of Salinguerra lineage.
>
> If his throat piece reached his chin
> he could conquer the seas, not to mention the lands;
> and whoever trembles and fears his face,
> isn't foolish nor mistaken, I believe.
>
> His face is ugly, his manner dangerous,
> and like a lion he roars frequently;
> whomever he fights would lose his coloring;
>
> and his eyes burn brightly like a lion's.
> I marvel greatly about his enemies —
> that they don't drop dead from the mere thought.

14. Quando Dïo messer Messerin fece
ben si credette far gran maraviglia,
ch'uccello e bestia ed uom ne sodisfece,
ch'a ciascheduna natura s'apiglia

ché nel gozzo anigrottol contrafece,
e ne le ren giraffa m'asomiglia,
ed uom sembia, secondo che si dice,[1]
ne la piagente sua cera vermiglia.

Ancor risembra corbo nel cantare,
ed è diritta bestia nel savere,
ed uomo è sumigliato al vestimento.

Quando Dio il fece, poco avea che fare,
ma volle dimostrar lo suo potere:
sì strana cosa fare ebbe in talento.

---

[1] Massèra and Vitale: 'dece'.

14. A sonnet about an ugly man, perhaps messer Messerino de' Caponsacchi, the uncle of Dante's love, Beatrice Portinari.

When God made messer Messerino
He thought he was making a great marvel;
He indulged bird and beast and man
because he shares the natures of all three:

because in his throat he mimics a duckling,
and in his flanks he resembles a giraffe,
and a man he seems, according to others,
in his ruddy and pleasant face.

And he also seems a crow when he sings,
and he's a true beast in his learning,
and a man he seems in his clothing.

When God made him He had little else to do,
but He wanted to display His power:
He desired to make such a strange thing.

15. Quando egli apre la bocca de la tomba
per dir parole, messer Casentino,
sì nel gozzo la boce gli rimbomba
che diserta le donne e guasta 'l vino.

E Baldanza si dorme, quando tromba,
ed hal per gica messere Ugolino:
ma quest'è il gran fastidio, che colomba
si crede che ver' sè fosse Merlino.
...

Sonnets 15–18: Deal with messer Ugolino. It may be that he was Ugolino di Bencivenne, about whom little is known. It is more likely that he was Ugolino degli Ubaldini, who sided with neither the Guelphs nor the Ghibellines out of political expediency; sonnet 17 describes messer Ugolino as playing one side off the other.

Sonnet 15 is fragmentary. In the manuscript it breaks off after the eighth line. The other individuals, messer Casentino and Baldanza, are unknown. The reference to Merlin is unclear, but it may allude to the idea that the wizard had a beautiful voice.

> When he opens his tomb-like mouth
> to utter words, messer Casentino
> has such a voice that echoes in his gullet —
> it scatters women and curdles wine.
>
> And Baldanza sleeps when he bellows,
> and Ugolino sees him as a trifle.
> But here's the annoying part: a dove
> was Merlin, he believes, compared to himself.

16. Le mie fanciulle gridan pur vivanda
e non finaro sera nè mattino,
e stanno tutte spesso in far domanda:
'Or nonn-è vivo messere Ugolino?'

Però ciascuna a voi si racomanda,
ed in ischiera v'è Lippo e Cantino,
che non temon che lor botte si spanda,
ché, s'han del pane, il pozzo è lor vicino.

Ond'io vi priego ancor, che[1] la speranza
daria per men di due fiorin lo staio,
ma le 'mpromesse atendo ad abondanza:

ch'a me penna non val né calamaio,
né me' venir né·ffar far ricordanza,
ned esser ricco più che Min di Ciaio.

---

[1] Massèra: 'ché'. In this instance, the translation follows Massèra's reading of 'ché' (because) rather than 'che' (which, that).

16. In addition to messer Ugolino, Rustico mentions Lippo, Cantino, and Min di Ciaio. Nothing is known about them.

Rustico stresses his own dire economic straits and discusses his daughters' suitors. Lippo and Cantino are willing to use up all the wine in their casks because they can substitute water from the well, Rustico writes.

Iacopo da Léona also mentions Rustico's daughters in a sonnet. Iacopo indicates that since Rustico doesn't have enough money for their dowries, he must rob from other people. Iacopo's sonnet also appears in this volume.

> My daughters holler out for food,
> and they don't stop morning or evening,
> and they crowd around asking this question:
> 'Is Ugolino no longer alive?'
>
> But each one commends herself to you,
> and in their group are Lippo and Cantino,
> who don't mind if the wine now flows from their casks[1]
> because if there's bread, there's always a well nearby.
>
> So I beg you again, for I have hope
> by the bushel that I'd sell for two florins;
> I fulfill my promises in abundance.
>
> But no pen or inkwell assists me,
> nor better reminders, nor memoranda,
> nor being richer than Min di Ciaio.

---

[1] Undoubtedly, the image of wine flowing from the men's casks has a second sexual connotation.

17. Chi messere Ugolin biasma o riprende
perché nonn-ha fermezza né misura
e perché sua promessa nonn-atende,
nonn-è cortese, ché·ll'ha da natura.

Ma fa gran cortesia chi 'l ne difende,
ch'è sì gentil che no ne mette cura,
e poco pensa se manca od offende,
e se vuol ben pensar, poco vi dura.

Ma i' so bene che, s'e' fosse leale,
ch'egli è di sì gran pregio il suo valore
che men se ne poria dir ben che male.

Ed ama la sua parte di bon core,
se non ch'a punto[1] ben no gliene cale,
e ben non corre a posta di signore.

---

[1] Massèra: 'punti'; Vitale: 'punt'i'.

17. This sonnet, which derides messer Ugolino as inconstant, gives some credence to the identification of him with Ugolino degli Ubaldini, who switched between the Guelph and Ghibelline causes during his lifetime.

Whoever blames or reproves Ugolino
because he lacks constancy and measure
or because he doesn't fulfill promises
isn't courteous — he's that way by nature.

Whoever defends him acts courteously
for he is so noble he needs no more nobility
and doesn't question if he fails or offends
and spends little time mulling how to act well.

But I know well if that person were loyal
because his valor is of such great worth,
he could say less good than ill about him,

and he loves his party with a good heart.
If not, at times, he cares for it not at all,
and he doesn't run at his master's bidding.

18. Io fo ben boto a Dio: se Ghigo fosse,
ser Cerbiolin, che·ll'hai tanto lodato,
per pillicion di quella c'ha le fosse,
non si riscalderia, tant'è gelato.

Non vedi che di mezzo luglio tosse
e 'l guarnel tien di sotto foderato?
E dicemi che fuoco anche nol cosse;
e' par figliuol di Bonella impiombato:

ché tutto il giorno sol seco si siede,
onde 'mbiecare ha·fatte molte panche,
se non ch'a manicare in casa riede.

Maraviglia che non gli cascar l'anche!
ché, se grande bisogno no·richiede,
da la sua casa no si partio anche.

18. The recipient of this sonnet, ser Cerbiolin, may have been Acerbo, the son of messer Attaviano dell'Acerbo (sonnets 6–8). Or he may have been Cerbiolin, son of Leale, who was exiled in 1268 for being a Ghibelline. Ghigo, the man who coughs and shivers, is unknown, as is his wife. Ghigo's coldness is due to the fact that his wife — a woman in possession of a 'pit' — doesn't share her 'pelt' with him; that is, she doesn't have sex with him. The reason is spelled out: he's so heavy that he appears to be made of lead.

The description of the woman's genitals as a pelt ('pillicion') appears based in the slang of the age. In the *Decameron* Giovanni Boccaccio repeatedly uses the same word with such a meaning (V, 10, 46; VIII, 7, 103; and X, 10, 69).

The idea of being sexually ignored resulting in an illness (because one is 'poorly covered' at night) is reiterated in sonnet 19. This sonnet influenced Dante, furthermore, who borrowed the notion of coughing in the summer to slander Forese Donati's wife, Nella. The exchange between Dante and Forese also appears in this volume.

> I make an oath to God: if Ghigo was,
> ser Cerbiolin, what you praised him to be,
> even with the pelt of the pitted woman,
> he wouldn't be heated, so cold is he.
>
> Don't you see that he coughs in mid-July,
> and he keeps his mantle stuffed in his lapel?
> And he tells me that not even fire cooks him;
> he appears the son of leadened Bonella;
>
> all day long he sits alone on his own;
> he has caused so many benches to warp,
> and he only returns home to eat.
>
> It's a marvel that his hips don't collapse!
> But, were it not that his great need requires it,
> he wouldn't even have left his house.

19. Se tu sia lieto di madonna Tana,
Azzuccio, dimmi s'io vertà ti dico;
e se tu no la veggi ancor puttana,
non ci guardar parente ned amico:

ch'io metto la sentenza in tua man piana,
e di neiente no la contradico,
perch'io son certo la darai certana;
non ne darei de l'altra parte un fico.

Ch'egli è più freddo che detto non aggio:
non vedi come 'l naso il manofesta?
ché redir non saprebbe di Cafaggio.

E spesse volte duolegli la testa;
Credo che stesse a balia ne Rimaggio:
tant'è salvaggio   pare una tempesta.

19. It is not known who Lady Tana or Azzuccio are. As in the previous sonnet, Azzuccio is sick because his wife doesn't have sex with him; she's probably having sex with someone else. Indeed, he's so ill that he couldn't make his way home from Cafaggio, a section of Florence. His illness is so bad that he seems to have been brought up in Rimaggio, a river that runs through Florence and therefore a very moist zone.

>If you are happy with Lady Tana,
>Azzuccio, tell me if I speak the truth:
>and if you don't see the whore that she is,
>don't turn to any relative or friend.
>
>Because I'll put the sentence clearly to you,
>and I won't contradict it for anything.
>I'm sure that you'll see it as certain,
>and I won't even bet a fig against it.
>
>He's colder than even I said he was.
>Can't you see how his runny nose shows it?
>He wouldn't know how to return from Cafaggio,
>
>and his head frequently causes him pain.
>He was under Rimaggio's influence;
>he's so wild that he seems a tempest.

20. Ne la stia mi par esser col leone
quando a Lutier son presso ad un migliaio,
ch'e' pute più che 'nfermo uom di pregione
o che nessun carname o che carnaio.

Li suo' cavegli farian fin buglione
e la cuffia faria ricco un oliaio
e li drappi de·lin bene a ragione
sarian per far panei[1] di quel massaio.

E' sente tanto di vivarra fiato
e di leonza e d'altro assai fragore,
mai nessun ne trovai sì smisurato;

ed escegli di sopra un tal sudore
che par veleno ed olio mescolato:
la rogna compie, s'ha mancanza fiore.

---

[1] Massèra and Marti: 'panel'; Vitale: 'panelli'.

20. It is unknown who this foul Lutieri was. See sonnet 7 for another reference to the smelliness of lions.

> I seem to be in the sty with a lion
> when I'm less than a mile from Lutieri,
> for he stinks more than a sick man in prison,
> or any rotten flesh or slaughterhouse.
>
> His hair would make a fine bouillon
> and his cap would make an oil-vender rich,
> and his linen mantel quite rightly
> would work well to make a cleaner's rags.
>
> And his breath smells strongly of civets,
> or of leopards, or other great stench —
> I've never come across one so extreme!
>
> And he's coated by the sweat he exudes
> that seems like a mixture of oil and venom:
> ringworm tops it off, if any more were needed.

21. Dovunque vai, con teco porti il cesso,
oi buggeressa vecchia puzzolente,
ché quale-unque persona ti sta presso
si tura il naso e fugge immantenente.

Li dent'i·le gengie tue ménar gresso
ché li taseva l'alito putente;
le selle paion legna d'alcipresso
inver' lo tuo fragor, tant'è repente.

Ché par che s'apran mille monimenta
quand'apri il ceffo; perché non ti spolpe
o ti rinchiude sì ch'om non ti senta?

Però che tutto 'l mondo ti paventa;
in corpo credo figlinti le volpe,
ta·lezzo n'esce fuor, sozza giomenta.

21. For centuries, the harangue against the old woman was a commonplace. The earliest example appears in Matthew of Vendôme's literary treatise (c. 1175), where he describes the offensive Beroë. Contemporaries of Rustico's who wrote similar sonnets included Guido Guinizzelli, Guido Cavalcanti and possibly Cecco Angiolieri.

Wherever you go, you bring the cesspool
with you old woman, smelly buggerer,
because whoever stands close to you
stops up his nose and flees right away.

Your teeth in your gums produce tartar
and a halitosis that stains them.
Asses seem fragrant like cypress wood
compared to your stench, it's so repulsive.

For it seems that a thousand crypts are opened
when you open your maw: why don't you drop dead
or close yourself off so no one can smell you?

But instead you frighten the whole world:
I think foxes breed inside your body
such a stench comes out, you filthy mare.

22. Al mio parer Teruccio non è grave,
ma scarso il tegno ismisuratamente;
e' ben cavalca de la man soave
quando d'avere utolità ne sente.

E con tale usa e vanno insieme·nave[1]
che boce glien'è corsa di mordente.
Non so se 'l fa, ma 'l suo sì serra a chiave
che 'l medesmo, che 'n tôrre è sì saccente,

non credo che del suo potesse avere.
Ch'è 'n questo è fermo il süo intendimento
del suo non dare, altrui tôrre a podere.

E se per rima fosse il suo lamento,
de' nuovi danni che stima d'avere
solazzi n'averemmo il giorno cento.

---

[1] Massèra, Marti, and Vitale: 'insieme 'n nave'.

22. About the cheapness — and thievery — of Teruccio. It is not known who this person was.

>In my opinion, Teruccio's not dull
>but, I believe, cheap beyond all measure;
>his hand rides softly over all things
>when he feels there's still some use for them.
>
>He frequents that other man, together they go,[1]
>so that biting rumors of them have spread:
>I don't know if he does it, but he locks up his things
>so the other one, who's wise about theft,
>
>can't carry off his stuff, I believe.
>Because his intention is firm in this:
>he won't give his, but will take others' by force.
>
>And if his complaint were written down in rhymes
>about all the new harm he thinks he's endured,
>we'd have one hundred days of entertainment

---

[1] Literally, 'they go together in a ship'.

23. Poi che guerito son de le mascelle
io no rido, ancor ch'i' smanio, e canto
che si sconciàr per rider di novelle
che mi contò Cristofan, dritto santo,

cui non bisogna colla e manovelle,
così le ti sciorina ad ogni canto;
e chi non si ralegrerà di quelle
in paradiso avrebbe doglie e pianto.

Oi Cion del Papa bene aventurato,
lasciati andar di man de lo sterlino,
credi a Cristofan ch'e' non è donato!

Per Dio, soccorri quel gentil Bandino,
ch'e' sia per te di morte sucitato:
è, ne le scritte, conte baladino.

23. Cristofan, Cion del Papa, and Bandino: it's not clear who these people are. But their hypocrisy, avarice and pretensions to nobility are well noted in this sonnet and the two that follow.

Since my jaws have now totally healed
I don't laugh, despite my desire — I sing.
They were shattered when I laughed at the news
that Cristofan, that upright saint, recounted.

It doesn't take instruments of torture
for him to piss it out on every corner —
and whoever doesn't rejoice hearing it
should feel pains and sorrows in heaven.

Oh Cion del Papa, so fortunate,
let some sterling silver out of your clutches —
trust in Cristofan, who gets no charity.

By God, give aid to noble Bandino
so that he will come back to life from death;
to judge from receipts, he's a paladin count.

24. Buono inconincio, ancora fosse veglio,
v'ebbe il valente messere Ubertino;
vostra grandezza va di bene in meglio,
ch'a voi ne viene il buon conte Bandino.

Quel da Romena, ch'è segnor del Peglio,
v'intende, so, cagion de lo sterlino;
e saccio ben, se moglie non ha il Veglio,
ch'e' gli assesini ha messi nel camino

per domandar la Diana o sua sorella;
ché quel da Senno nonn-è tanto ardito
ch'egli oggi adomandasse la fancella.

E Tanuccio n'è molto isbigottito
e nonn-ha più speranza in suo' castella;
né 'l cardinal, secondo ch'aggio udito.

24. In addition to featuring Bandino and possibly Cione del Papa from the previous sonnet, this one also includes the noblemen Ubertino degli Ubaldini, Ugolino degli Ubaldini ('the one from Senno'), Count Guido of Romena ('lord of Peglio'), and Tanuccio degli Ubaldini. They are all vying for the hand of Cione's daughter Diana, who also appears in the following sonnet.

As in sonnet 12 Rustico alludes to the legend of the Old Man of the Mountain, who controlled the band of assassins.

>A good beginning, even though he's now old,
>did valiant messer Ubertino have;
>your greatness goes from good to better
>since good count Bandino comes to stay with you.
>
>One from Romena, who's lord of Peglio
>heeds you, I know, because of your sterling:
>I know well, if no wife does the Old Man have
>who sent the assassins along the road,
>
>by requesting to ask for Diana or her sister;
>because the one from Senno isn't so brave
>since today he asked for that servant girl.
>
>And Tanuccio has lost all courage
>and he has no faith in his castles;
>neither does the cardinal, from what I hear.

25. Il giorno avesse io mille marchi d'oro
che la Dianuzza fia contessa Diana,
e sanza grande isfolgòr di tesoro;
e non cavaleressa né cattana.

È fermo più che 'l genovese moro
lo detto di Cristofano in Toscana;
e poi apresso, sanza gran dimoro,
farem de l'altra orrevol marchisciana.

Fra gli altri partiremo li casati:
Donati ed Adimar sia del Capraccia;
di Donaton, Tosinghi e Giandonati.

Se più ve n'ha che non sian maritati,
dean la parola là ove più lor piaccia:
e se rilievo v'ha, sia degli Abati.

25. As in the previous sonnets, Cristofano and Diana appear here. As before, Rustico derides the pretenders to Diana's hand in marriage. In this sonnet, though, he also criticizes her social-climbing: with enough money, she could claim to be a countess. Rustico then discusses the marital arrangements of the children of Capraccia and Donatoni. They, too, can be married into such powerful Florentine families as the Donati, Adimari, Tosinghi, Giandonati, and the Abati.

> The day I had a thousand gold marks
> Dianuzza would be countess Diana
> without the great glinting of treasure;
> not even chevaleresse or captain.
>
> More solid than the pier of Genoa
> is the word of Cristofano in Tuscany;
> then, without delay, we'll make the other sister
> into an honorable marquise.
>
> Among the rest we'll divide up the houses:
> Donati and Adimari for Capraccia;
> for Donaton, Tosinghi and Giandonati.
>
> And if you have more unmarried children,
> they should give their word to whomever they want.
> And if more come, they'll go to the Abati.

26. Da che guerra m'avete incominciata,
palesarò del vostro puttineccio,
de la foia, che tanto v'è montata
che non s'atuteria per pal di·lleccio.

Non vi racorda, donna, a la fïata
che noi stemmo a San Sebio in tal gineccio?
E se per moglie v'avesse sposata,
non dubbiate ch'egli era un bel farneccio.

Che foste putta il die che voi nasceste
ed io ne levai saggio ne la stalla:
ché 'l culo in terra tosto percoteste,

e sed io fosse stato una farfalla,
maraviglia saria, sì mi scoteste:
voi spingate col cul, quando altri balla.

26. It is unknown who the recipient of this sonnet was, nor the identity of Chierma in sonnet 27. In the thirteenth century Rustico was renowned as a misogynistic writer, frequently using women's sexuality to slander them. Nowhere is that clearer than in these sonnets. In thirteenth- and fourteenth-century Italy prostitutes were reputed to have sex with their clients in stalls; thus, Rustico implies that she is a prostitute as well.

Since you've declared war against me
I'll make your whorishness perfectly plain
and your horniness, which has so increased
that it couldn't be reined in with an oak branch.

Don't you remember, woman, that time
when we made a whorehouse of San Sebio?
And if I'd married you as my wife,
don't doubt that it would have been insanity

since you've been a whore since the day you were born:
that was made clear to me in the stall
as you smacked your ass against the ground.

And if I'd been as light as a butterfly
it would have been amazing, you shook me so.
You bump with your ass, while your partner 'dances'.

27. A voi, Chierma, so dire una novella:
se voi porrete il culo al colombaio,
cad io vi porgerò tal manovella,
se non vi piace, io non ne vo' danaio.

Ma tornerete volontier per ella,
ch'ella par drittamente d'un somaio:
con tutto che non siate sì zitella
che troppo colmo paiavi lo staio.

Adunque, Chierma, non ci date indugio,
che pedir vi farabbo come vacca
se porrete le natiche al pertugio.

Tutte l'altre torrete poi per acca:
sì vi rinzafferò col mio segugio
ch'e' parrà ch'Arno v'esca de la tacca.

27. It is unknown who this woman Chierma was. But this is another example of Rustico decrying women's sexuality.

> I know how to tell you a story, Chierma:
> if you bring your ass to the dovecote
> I'll stick you with such a cattle prod —
> if you don't like it, you won't have to pay me.
>
> But you'll return willingly for it,
> because it rightly resembles a donkey's;
> and for as much as you aren't a virgin
> your bushel will seem overly full.
>
> Therefore, Chierma, make no delay:
> because I'll make you fart like a cow
> if you bring your buttocks to the dovecote.
>
> All the others will seem worthless as an 'h'.
> I'll so chase you down with my hunting dog
> it'll seem the Arno flows out your notch.

28. Quando ser Pepo vede alcuna potta
egli anitrisce sì come distriere
e no sta queto: inanzi salta e trotta
e canzisce che par pur un somiere;

e com' baiardo ad ella si ragrotta
e ponvi il ceffo molto volontiere,
ed ancor de la lingua già non dotta
e spesse volte mordele il cimiere.

Chi vedesse ser Pepo incavallare
ed anitrir, quando sua donna vede,
che si morde le labbra e vuol razzare,

quelli, che dippo par non si ricrede:
quando v'ha 'l ceffo sì la fa sciacquare,
sì le stringe la groppa ch'ella pede.

28. It may be that this sonnet is about Pepo Rinaldeschi, a notary, or Pepo Adimari, a guarantor for the Guelphs in 1280. Or it is possible that Pepo is simply a metaphor for the penis. Rustico compares Pepo's reactions to horses, even alluding to Bayard, the great steed of the warrior Roland.

> When ser Pepo looks upon any cunt
> he whinnies just like a charger
> and he's not quiet: rather he jumps and trots
> and becomes foolish so he seems a donkey.
>
> And like Bayard he sidles up to her
> and he most willingly gives her his muzzle;
> and he doesn't restrain his tongue;
> and he often nips her on the crest.
>
> Whoever saw ser Pepo horsing
> and whinnying when he sees his lady —
> he bites his lip and tries to mount her.
>
> What he seems next, no one will believe:
> while he holds his muzzle he rinses her off,
> and he so clutches her haunches that she farts.

29. El Muscia sì fa dicere e bandire,
qual donna non avesse buon marito,
ch'aggia picciol dificio da servire,
che vada a·llui, cad e' n'è ben fornito.

Ed ancor questo fa nel bando dire,
ch'è sedici once, sanza i·rimonito;
e dice ben, se no la fa pedire
a ogni tratto, ch'e' vuol perdere lo 'nvito.

Ma se se ne aterranno al mio consiglio,
inanzi il proveranno ver' di mezzo,[1]
que' c'ha la schiena bianca e 'l co vermiglio;

e poi, quando verrà colà 'l da sezzo,
darannovi con ambo man di piglio,
ch'a ben ripalleggiarlo egli è un vezzo.

---

[1] Marrani: 'verdemézzo'.

29. A sonnet about Niccola Muscia, who wrote love poetry for a man, Lano. Muscia was also criticized by Iacomo de' Tolomei for his homosexuality. The verses of Niccola Muscia and Iacomo de' Tolomei also appear in this volume.

> Muscia inspires talk and proclamations:
> whichever woman has a bad husband,
> for he has a small tower to serve her with,
> should go to him because he's well furnished.
>
> And he also makes this be announced:
> it weighs sixteen ounces without any extras;
> and he says that if he doesn't make them fart
> with every thrust, he won't take the bet.
>
> But unless the women heed my counsel,
> they will sooner find flaccid that which
> has a white back and a vermillion head;
>
> and then, when they arrive at that point,
> they will grab it with both of their hands,
> for to shake it well is such a delight!

30.[1] Vogliendo contentarmi[2] di composte,
la dona mia si tolse la cispa d'ochi:
erave manti e zimizi e pidochi,
e rogna, schianze di tign'a le coste.

E poscia, tosto che foron[3] riposte
in sella, ov'è anche di merda rochi,
mignate e vermi colse per finochi,
e sì ne puose bene in cento poste.

Quando le cose furono assettate,[4]
vi fece su versare una postema,
e piscio puzolente una bigonça,

e ricetar tre dì còlora e rema;
poi disce: 'mangia de le composte'; aconcia
mochi e scarca, sì di gra' van salate.'[5]

---

[1] Cited from the edition by Giuseppe Marrani, 'I sonetti di Rustico Filippi', *Studi di filologia italiana* 57 (1999), 33–196. Federici provided a reading of the sonnet that more closely followed the manuscript; see Vincenzo Federici, *Le rime di Rustico di Filippo rimatore fiorentino del sec. XIII* (Bergamo: Arti Grafiche, 1889).
[2] Federici: 'contentarla'.
[3] Federici: 'foson'.
[4] Federici: 'assentite'.
[5] Federici: 'vassallaci'.

30. This sonnet is considered apocryphal by many critics. It is the only one not found in the thirteenth-century Vatican Latin 3793 manuscript, but in the fifteenth-century codex Vatican Urbinati 697. In Rustico's other sonnets, he slanders women and he crafts offensive descriptions of other people; but none approaches the vileness of this sonnet.

> Desiring to please me with a *compote*,
> my lady pulled the rheum from her eyes;
> there were also many bedbugs and lice,
> and scabies and ringworm, scabs on her eyelids.
>
> And then, once all these things were placed
> on the toilet seat, with morsels of shit,
> she gathered bloodsuckers and worms like fennels
> and put them in a hundred dishes.
>
> When the ingredients were all prepared,
> she poured over them a vile cesspool
> and a full bucket of stinking piss,
>
> and three days' worth of bile and catarrh,
> and she said: 'eat this *compote*'; then she arranged
> snot and waste, for they should be seasoned so.

31. Amor fa nel mio cor fermo soggiorno
e quindi non si parte né va fori,
ma manda li suo' messi spesso intorno
cercando e provedendo gli amadori.

E 'ntende le ragion ciaschedun giorno:
a tal dà gioia, a tal dona dolori;
ma 'l meo Segnore ha me in tal loco adorno
ch'io passo tutti gli altri intenditori.

Oi core orrato più di nessun core,
perch'ami la megliore e la più gente;
orrato, poi che torna teco Amore!

Cortese ed amoroso meo Segnore,
di cui mi credo star leal servente,
non vi so graze far di tanto onore.

31. The phenomenology of Love, which resides in the lover's heart.

>Love makes a firm sojourn in my heart
>and from there he never departs or goes out;
>he sends out his messengers all around,
>seeking out other lovers and providing for them.
>
>And every day he hears their reasons:
>to one he gives joy, to another great pains.
>But my lord does me such honor in my heart
>that I surpass all who understand him.
>
>Oh, heart honored more than any other heart,
>you love the best and most gentle woman;
>honored, because love always returns to you.
>
>My courteous and amorous Lord,
>whose loyal servant I will always remain,
>I don't know how to repay you for such honor.

32. Tutte le donne ch'io audo laudare,
parmi che lor non aggiano bieltate;
quando posso la mia donna membrare
son neiente le laude che son date:

ma' che vorria ch'Amor tanto in parlare
mi desse graza ch'io con veritate
savesse a tutta gente adimostrare
com'è somma de l'altre donne nate.

Dëo, che maraviglia sembreria
a dir tanta smisura di bellezze
quante son quelle di madonna mia!

Perch'io non posso dir le grand'altezze;
io non so se m'aven per gelosia
ch'io nonn-oso nomar le sue adornezze.

32. The beauty of all other women is surpassed by that of the beloved. She is so lovely that the poet cannot fully express it. A fine lover is supposed to be jealous of everyone, and the poet's jealousy prevents him from describing the lady.

> All the women that I hear being praised
> seem to me as having no beauty at all.
> When I call back my lady to mind
> the praises of them seem nothing at all.
>
> Above all, I wish that Love, when I speak,
> granted me such grace that, honestly,
> I knew how to demonstrate to everyone
> how she is the highest woman ever born.
>
> God, what a marvel it would seem to me
> if I could relate such extreme beauty
> as the beauty that my lady has.
>
> Therefore I cannot relate her highest station.
> I don't know if it's my jealousy
> but I don't even dare to mention her graces.

33. Come pote la gente soferire,
donna amorosa, standovi lontana?
Chi vive como si puote partire
da la vostra gioiosa cera umana?

Ben me ne maraviglio, a lo ver dire,
ché de le donne siete la sovrana.
Come si trova i·llor tanto fallire
ched a·llor non istate prossimana?

Eo nol dico, madonna, che mi doglia
di questo fallo che la gente face:
paremi così gran maraviglia.

E so ben che non fora vostra voglia,
e me dismisuratamente piace:
tanta di gelosia l'Amor m'apiglia.

33. Rustico describes her as the sovereign of all ladies.

> How's it possible for people to endure,
> lovely lady, staying far away from you?
> Whoever is living, how can he depart
> from your joyful and humane face?
>
> I marvel greatly, to tell you the truth,
> for you are the sovereign of all ladies.
> How can such failings be found in others
> that you won't even be found near to them?
>
> My lady, I don't say that I'm pained
> by the failings that other people have:
> it seems to be a great marvel to me.
>
> I know well that it wouldn't be your desire;
> and I like it beyond all measure —
> so much jealousy does Love cause me.

34. I' aggio inteso che sanza lo core
non pò l'om viver né durar neiente;
ed io vivo sanz'esso, e lo colore
però non perdo, né saver, né mente:

ma solo per la forza del Segnore
che 'l n'ha portato, che, tanto potente,
lo dipartì dal corpo, ciò fue Amore:
e' l'ha miso in balìa de l'avenente.

Lo cor, quando dal corpo si partio,
disse ad Amor: 'Segnore, in quale parte
mi meni?' E que' rispose: 'Al tuo disio.'

'In tale loco è che già mai no parte';
insieme sta il meo core e 'l disir mio:
così vi fosse il corpo in terza parte!

34. The lordship of Love, which takes possession of the lover's heart.

    I always understood that without a heart
    a man cannot live nor endure a moment;
    I live without it, and yet my color
    doesn't fade, nor do I lose wisdom or thought;

    it's by the Lord's power — he was Love —
    that removed it, for he's so powerful
    that he separated it from my body
    and left it in the lovely lady's care.

    My heart, when it left from my body, asked Love:
    'Lord, where are you leading me?'
    And he responded: 'To your desire:

    to that place, and never departs from it.'
    My heart and my desire are together —
    if only my body were the third one there!

35. Madonna, quando eo voi non veggio in viso
tant'è forte e dogliosa la mia pena
che 'n su la morte mi conduce e mena,
non m'aucide e tenemi conquiso.

E quando eo sto da voi, bella, diviso,
languisco se l'Amor non mi rimena;
e 'l vostro bel riguardo mi dà lena
e mi ritien ch'io non mi sono auciso.

Volete audire, amor, gentil penzero
per ch'io donare a me morte non voglio?
che dico: 'Con' vedrei poi 'l viso clero?'

E sed io nol vedesse com'io soglio,
come faria? Però non mi dispero.
Amor, merzé, che tanto aggio d'orgoglio.

35. The trope of *amor de lohn*, or the suffering of the lover when he is distant from the lady.

> My lady, whenever I don't see your face
> my pain is so dolorous and so fierce
> that it leads me — it drives me — ever toward death
> but it doesn't kill me; it holds me captive.
>
> And, Beauty, when I'm separated from you
> I languish if Love doesn't lead me back to you.
> And your beautiful image gives me courage
> and holds me back from just ending my life.
>
> Do you want to hear, Love, the gentle thought
> for which I don't want to give myself to Death?
> I say: 'How would I then see her bright face?'
>
> If I didn't see it, as I often do,
> what would I do? Thus, I don't despair.
> Have mercy, Love, for such pride that I feel!

36. Dovunque eo vo o vegno o volgo o giro,
a voi son, donna mia, tuttor davanti,
e s'eo co·gli occhi altrove guardo o miro,
lo cor non v'è, poi ch'io faccio i sembianti.

E spesse volte sì forte sospiro
che par che 'l cor dal corpo mi si schianti:
alor piango e lamento, e non m'adiro,
ma li mei occhi bagno tutti quanti;

e dolzemente faccio mio cordoglio,
tuttor , mia donna, a voi merzé chiamando
umilemente più quant'eo più doglio.

Durar non posso più disiderando;
non aggio di voi quello ch'aver soglio:
morrò per voi piangendo e sospirando.

36. The lady's image has been imprinted on the lover's soul. The memory of her beauty continually stimulates his desire, leaving him in a state of perpetual pain.

> Wherever I go or come or turn or travel
> I am always, my lady, before you;
> and if with my eyes I glance or stare elsewhere
> my heart isn't there, for this is just pretense.
>
> And very often I sigh so strongly
> that my heart seems to break from my body;
> then I weep and lament, but I don't feel wrath —
> I dampen my eyes so completely.
>
> And sweetly I express my heartache,
> all the while, my lady, begging for mercy
> ever more humbly, as my torment grows.
>
> I can't endure this desire much longer;
> I don't have from you what I'm used to having.
> I will die crying and sighing for you.

37. Merzé, madonna, non mi abandonate,
e non vi piaccia ch'io stessi m'aucida;
poi che venne da voi questa amistate,
dovetemi esser donna, porto e guida.

Durar non posso più, se mi tardate
conven per ben la morte mi conquida.
Oi amorosa somma di bieltate,
piacciavi ch'io diporti e giochi e rida.

In voi è la mia morte e la mia vita:
oi, donna mia, traetemi di pene;
se nol fate, la vita a mort'è gita.

E se di me, madonna, a voi sovene,
la mia faccia dogliosa e scolorita
ritornerà 'n istato di gran bene.

37. The lover's plea that the lady shouldn't ignore his pains.

>Mercy, my lady, don't abandon me,
>and it shouldn't please you that I should kill myself;
>since this friendliness first came from you,
>you should be my lady, my haven, and guide.
>
>I can't endure longer — if you delay
>it will happen that death conquers me.
>Oh, amorous heights of comeliness,
>may it please you that I play, joke, and laugh.
>
>In you resides both my death and my life.
>Oh, my lady, take me from this torment —
>for if you don't, my life will turn to death.
>
>And if you, my lady, remember me,
>my dolorous and discolored face
>will return to its state of great goodness.

38. Amore, onde vien l'acqua che lo core
agli occhi senza mai rifinar manda?
Saria per tuo comandamento, Amore?
Eo credo ben che mova a tua dimanda.

E' pare a me che surgia di dolore,
e convien che con duol degli occhi spanda;
ché, se dagli occhi non uscisse fore,
lo cor morria: Amor no lo comanda.

Amor non vol ch'io moia, ma languendo
viva: così cortese segnoria
mi faccia Amor, po' ch'io non mi difendo.

In quest'è tutta la speranza mia:
che tanto le starò merzé cherendo,
che sia pietosa più sua segnoria.

38. The traditional image of the lover as continually weeping.

> Love, whence comes the water that the heart
> sends to my eyes without ever ending?
> Does it happen because of your command?
> I believe that it moves at your request.
>
> It seems to me that it arises from pain
> and necessarily expands at the eyes;
> for if it didn't exit from the eyes
> the heart would die — this, Love doesn't command.
>
> Love doesn't want me to die, but to live
> languishing; so may Love be courteous in his lordship,
> since I don't defend myself.
>
> In this one thing resides all my hope:
> I will go on begging her for mercy
> so that her lordship will be more humane.

39. L'afanno e 'l gran dolor ch'io meco porto
mi dovria mille fiate avere auciso;
ma per la dismisura non son morto,
che men dolor m'avria morto e conquiso:

ch'io son degli smarruti capo e porto,
sì come d'ogni gioia paradiso:
adunque chi ha pena e disconforto
comeco i·nullo logo sia conmiso.

Per ch'io voglio esser de l'altrui mal miro,
e voglio a ciaschedun dar guerigione
veggendo lo mio pianto e lo sospiro.

Non avranno mai dol né pensagione,
tant'è lo male ch'io comeco tiro:[1]
perché de me' morir nonn-è stagione.

---

[1] Buzzetti Gallarati: 'comeco 'n tiro'.

39. An expression of the lover's extreme pain.

> The torment and the great suffering I bear
> should have killed me a thousand times over;
> but because it's so extreme I didn't die,
> since less pain would have conquered and killed me.
>
> I'm the leader and refuge of lost people,
> just as heaven is the greatest of all joys;
> therefore, whoever has pain or discomfort
> shouldn't be compared to me in any way.
>
> I want to doctor other people's pain[1]
> and I want to give cures to everyone
> who sees my weeping and my sighing.
>
> They will never have pains or heavy thoughts:
> such is the pain I bring along with me
> since it isn't the time for me to die.

---

[1] Literally, 'I want to be the example (*miro*) for other people's pain'.

40. Tant'è lo core meo pien di dolore
e tant'è forte la doglia ch'eo sento,
ca s'e' de la mia pena mi lamento
la lingua il dice sì, che par dolzore.

A me foria mistier che lo mio core
parlasse, ch'e' mostrasse il suo tormento:
eo credo certo, sanza fallimento,
ca di pietà ne piangerebbe Amore.

Oi core meo e occhi, che farete?
Cor, come soferrai dolor cotanto?
ed occhi, voi che sì spesso piangete?

Amor, merzé, ch'aleni lo mio pianto;
e voi, per Dio, madonna, provedete
che lo dolor del cor ritorni in canto.

40. An expression of the lover's pain, with the plea for the lady to help him.

> My heart is so full of suffering
> and so strong is the pain that I feel
> that if I complain about my torment
> my tongue speaks and it seems as sweetness.
>
> It should be necessary for my heart
> to speak itself and show its own torment;
> I believe with certainty, without fail,
> that Love would weep for it out of pity.
>
> Oh, my heart and eyes, what will you do?
> Heart, how will you ever endure such pain?
> And eyes, why do you cry so frequently?
>
> Mercy, Love, so may my tears be lessened.
> And you, my lady, by God see to it
> that my heart's suffering turns into song.

41   Similmente la notte come 'l giorno
io dormo e poso e ho sollazzo e gioco,
e simile mi volgo e giro intorno
e sto, senza pensier doglioso, poco;

e spesse volte a pianger mi ritorno
e quindi bagno l'amoroso foco,
e lo pensiero e 'l pianto è 'l mio soggiorno:
oi lasso, che tutto ardo e 'ncendo e coco!

E nessun foco   mai cangia calore
o che faccia languire o tormentare,
per certo non, con' fa il foco d'Amore,

che 'l natural ti fa poco durare:
ma quegli ha vita, ca più tosto more,
a cui no vole Amore allegro fare.

41. Rustico compares the pains of love to the pains of fire. Fire kills its victim quickly, but the lover lives on in torment.

>During both the night and day equally
>I sleep and rest, and have pleasure and play,
>and likewise I turn and travel about
>and I pass little time without painful thoughts.
>
>Often times I turn back to my weeping
>and thus I wet the amorous fire,
>and the thoughts and tears are my repose —
>oh, alas, I burn and flame and blaze.
>
>And no fire ever changes its heat
>or causes such weakness or torment,
>certainly not in the way love's fire does.
>
>Natural fire kills you quite quickly
>but this one leaves alive, rather than killing,
>whoever Love doesn't want to make happy.

42. Amore, a voi domando perdonanza,
sì como fin servente al suo segnore,
s'eo dico cosa che vi si' a pesanza,
ché soferir non pò la doglia il core.

Sacciate che segnor sanza pietanza
tanto non val, con' s'ha pietoso il core.
Oimè, che dissi! Forse che fallanza
terrà che 'nver di·llui dett'aggia Amore.

Vengianza, se fallato aggio, ne prenda,
ché la pena m'incalcia e dà conforto
ch'io dica, e poco pensa ch'io misprenda.

Però perdon dovria trovar del torto;
ma prego la ragion che mi difenda
e de l'altezza mi conduca a porto.

42. The poet presents himself as a servant of Love. He begs for pity, hoping that his lord will end his torment.

>Love, I will beg you for forgiveness
>as a fine servant does of his lord,
>if I say anything that weighs upon you
>because my heart can't endure its pain.
>
>You know that a pitiless lord's worth
>doesn't equal one whose heart feels pity.
>Alas! What have I said? Perhaps Love
>will consider what I've said as a failing.
>
>He should seek vengeance if I have failed him,
>because my pain encourages me to speak
>and comforts me, and he doesn't notice when I err.
>
>But pardon should be offered for my mistake
>and I pray that reason should defend me
>and should lead me from the high sea to the port.

43. Tutto lo giorno intorno vo fuggendo,
credendomi campar, davanti Amore,
e s'io trovo nessun, forte piangendo
lo prego che mi celi al mio Segnore.

Oi lasso, con' gran pene soferendo
condotto ho me medesmo in questo errore!
ché, quando i' sono assai gito languendo,
io trovo Amor che m'è dentro dal core.

Così la pena c'ho mi mena e caccia,
che mi fa soferir l'amore amaro,
che spesso il giorno il cor m'arde ed aghiaccia.

E non mi manca pena, ched io saccia;
lo mal m'è vile e 'l ben m'è troppo caro:
Amor, merzé, ch'io non so ch'io mi faccia.

43. The cruel lordship of Love.

> All day long I go fleeing here and there
> believing I can survive before Love,
> and if I find anyone, weeping hard
> I beg him to hide me from my lord.
>
> Oh alas, how have I, suffering so,
> led myself to this wandering?
> For when I've gone to great lengths languishing
> I find Love, who's within my own heart.
>
> I'm led and driven by the pain I have,
> which bitter Love causes me to suffer,
> and my heart burns and freezes through the day.
>
> There's no pain I don't have, that I know of —
> this evil's bad for me, this goodness too dear —
> mercy, Love, for I don't know what to do.

44. Amor, poi che del mio mal non vi dole,
 più siete inver' di me fero che fera;
 Amor, guardate inver' le mie parole:
 s'aggio fallato, piacciavi ch'io pèra.

 E s'io nonn-ho mancato, come sole
 lo mio cor ritornate a quella spera,
 che tanto quanto guarda o gira il sole
 più doglioso di me merzé non chera.

 Oi Morte, chi t'apella 'dura Morte'
 non sente ciò ched io patisco e sento,
 ché, se mi vuoli aucider, mi conforte;

 ché la mia vita passa ogni tormento.
 Oi Morte, perché l'arma non ne porte
 e falla far dal secol partimento?

44. The lover calls on Death to end his suffering at the hands of Love.

>Love, since my ill causes you no pain
>you are more fierce to me than a wild beast;
>Love, look at my words: if I've failed you
>then may it please you for me to die.
>
>If I haven't failed you, as is usual
>you should return my heart to its place,
>because nothing that sees the light of the sun
>and calls for mercy is more pained than me.
>
>Oh, Death, whoever calls you 'Hard Death'
>doesn't feel what I suffer and feel
>since if you killed me, you'd comfort me
>
>because my life surpasses all torment.
>Oh Death, why don't you draw your arms
>and separate my life from this world?

45. A nessuno omo adivenne già mai
ch'Amor prendesse altrui sanza veduta;
a meve è adivenuto; non pensai
ca sì forte pungesse sua feruta.

Ch'e' mi tormenta e dona pena assai,
se madonna amorosa non m'aiuta,
che m'ha in balìa; ed io medesmo il sai,
che·ll'ho donato il cor sanza partuta.

Dunque mi dé' campare, ed a ragione:
qualunque buon segnore a suo servente,
che·llui ha messa tutta sua intenzone,

non dé' sofrir ch'e' moia di neiente,
ché·lli sarabbe grande riprensione:
questo fedel son io, donna valente.

45. Love's unjust treatment of his servant, the lover.

> To no other man has it ever happened
> that Love took him without his being aware:
> to me it happened; I didn't believe
> that his wounds would sting me so harshly.
>
> For he torments me and gives me great pain —
> if my amorous lady doesn't help me,
> for she has me in her power; and I know it
> because I've given her my entire heart.
>
> Therefore she should save me, and rightly so —
> any good lord, regarding his servant
> who has put all his good will in him
>
> should not allow him to die for nothing.
> To do so would be a great reproach to him.
> I am that faithful one, valiant lady.

46. Unqua per pene ch'io patisca amando,
lasso, già non vorria disamorare:
omè, che per aver disiderando,
ciò ch'io sostegno non porria[1] mostrare.

Ché solo pur le lagrime ch'io spando
sovente fannomi maravigliare;
e quanto più languisco e vo penando,
alor[2] si ferma il cor meo più d'amare.

E s'ïo ardisse d'incolpare Amore,
eo diceria ch'avesse di me torto,
dapoi che fuor di me nonn-è[3] dolore.

Se non che spero ancor d'aver conforto,
là dov'è grande pregio e gran valore:
sol è colpa d'Amor s'io pene porto.

---

[1] Massèra, Marti, and Vitale: 'poria'.
[2] Massèra, Marti, and Vitale: 'allor'.
[3] Massèra, Marti, and Vitale: 'non è'.

46. The lover's desire to remain enamored in spite of his torment.

>Despite the pains I suffer by loving,
>alas, I wouldn't want to fall out of love;
>oh me, what I endure by desiring
>I could never demonstrate to anyone.
>
>Because just the amount of tears I shed
>frequently causes me to marvel;
>and the more that I languish and suffer
>the more my heart is firm in its love.
>
>And if I dared to put the blame on Love
>I would say that he was the one at fault
>since, compared to mine, no other pain exists.
>
>If not that I still hope to feel solace
>in that woman who has great worth and valor:
>it is only Love's fault that I feel pain.

47. Ispesse volte voi vegno a vedere
per sodisfare agli occhi ed a lo core;
ma quand'eo parto sì mi stringe Amore
ch'io non saccio che via deggia tenere.

E di tornar mi sforza lo volere
sì m'ha 'nfiammato Amor del suo calore;
e poi, quando mi parto, lo dolore
alor ritorna, e partesi il piacere.

Adunque, lasso, como deggio fare?
Ch'io non posso tuttor madonna mia
veder co·gli occhi, e 'l cor fare alegrare.

Gentile ed amorosa più che sia,
e sai in che guisa tu mi puoi campare:
non pèra sanza gioia, ch'io non dovria.

47. The lover's perpetual suffering.

>Many times I come to look at you
>to satisfy my eyes and my heart;
>and when I depart, Love assaults me[1]
>so I don't know which way I should take.
>
>And he forces me to want to return,
>Love has so inflamed me with his heat;
>And then, when I leave, the suffering
>returns again and all pleasure leaves me.
>
>Therefore, alas, how should I behave?
>Because I can't look upon my lady
>at all hours with my eyes and please my heart.
>
>Gentle, lovely lady beyond all others
>you know in which way you can save me;
>I shouldn't die joyless — I don't deserve it.

[1] Literally, 'love constrains me'.

48. Sì tosto con' da voi, bella, partuto
son, mantenente ritornar vorria;
e sentome mortalmente feruto,
perdo la conoscenza e·lla balìa.

Ma sì non perdo ch'io no speri aiuto
di voi, gentil più ch'altra che mai sia:
ch'io son fedel d'Amor tanto vivuto
a la speranza di voi, donna mia.

Sì come il partimento mi dà noia,
amorosa e gentil donna piagente,
così è·ritornar somma di gioia.

E se non fosse l'anoiosa gente,
la qual disia che doloroso moia,
eo viveria per voi alegramente.

48. The suffering of the lover finding himself distant from the lady (*amor de lohn*).

>As quickly as I left, Beauty, from you,
>so immediately do I want to return,
>and I feel myself mortally wounded.
>I lose my consciousness and self-control.
>
>I'm not so far gone I don't hope for help
>from you, who are nobler than all others.
>For I have lived as Love's faithful servant
>placing my hope in you, my dear lady.
>
>And just as my departure hurts me,
>lovely and pleasing gentle woman,
>so returning is the height of joy.
>
>And were it not for the hateful people
>who want me to die painfully,
>I would live joyfully just for you.

49. Io non auso rizzar, chiarita spera,
inver' voi gli occhi, tant' ho gelosia,
e feremi nel viso vostra spera,
e gli occhi abasso e non so là ove sia.

Oi amorosa ed avenante cera,
non mi tardate la speranza mia,
ch'ad onta de la gente malparliera
mi riterrete in vostra segnoria.

Deo, como son lontan da me' pensiero
li falsi e li noiosi maldigenti,
che là non volgo l'arco ov'eo ne fero;

ma tutavia mi fan sofrir tormenti,
ché spesso l'amoroso viso clero
s'asconde per li falsi parlamenti.

49. The jealousy of the lover, and his disdain for the gossips who ruin love affairs (*lauzengiers*).

> I don't dare to lift up, shining ray,
> my eyes toward you, I feel so jealous;
> and when your resplendence strikes my face
> I lower my eyes and I feel lost.
>
> Oh, amorous and beautiful face,
> do not delay in the hope I bear:
> in spite of the people who speak ill
> you will retain me in your dominion.
>
> God, how distant from my own thoughts
> are the false and hateful people who speak ill
> because I don't strike them with my bow.
>
> But yet they cause me to suffer pain
> because the resplendent face frequently
> hides itself thanks to their ill speech.

50. Quant'io verso l'Amor più m'umilìo,
a me più mostra fera segnoria;
e più monta e cresce il meo disio,
e più mi tien doglioso notte e dia.

Adunque, lasso, como faraggio io,
se non mi soccorrete, donna mia?
Se mi tardate, bella, lo cor mio
durar non pò più vita, anzi va via.

Ciascun mi guarda in viso e fa dimando,
veggendomi cangiato lo visaggio;
ed io celo la doglia mia in parlando,

e non ardisco dir lo meo coraggio,
perch'io l'ho da la mia donna in comando.
Oi lasso, ch'attendendo mi[1] morraggio!

---

[1] Massèra, Marti, and Vitale omit 'mi'.

50. The cruel lordship of Love, and the lover's plea to the lady.

>The more I humble myself before Love,
>the more he treats me with fierce lordship;
>and the more my desire mounts and grows
>the more he keeps me in pain night and day.
>
>Therefore, alas, whatever will I do
>if you do not save me, my lady?
>If you cause my heart to delay, Beauty,
>my life won't last — instead it wastes away.
>
>Everyone looks at my face and wonders
>seeing how my face has been changed:
>and I hide my pain when I am speaking.
>
>And I don't dare to express my heart
>because my lady has commanded it —
>oh me, I will surely die while waiting.

51. Tanto di cor verace e fino amante
i' son, madonna, inver' di voi stato,
che quando fosse a voi, cor me', davante,
eo non pensava d'esservi incolpato.

E s'io facea davanti altrui sembiante,
già non credea di nulla esser guardato;
ond'io doglie ne porto e pene tante
che morte vita mi sarebbe in grato.

Qual uomo ama di cor perfettamente
nonn-ha mai conoscenza né misura,
tant'è lo foco de l'amore ardente.

E se per nulla cangiasi natura,
sì fa per gli amadori veracemente,
tant'è lor condizion dogliosa e dura.

51. The lover's plea to the lady.

>Of such a true heart, and a fine lover
>my lady, have I been toward you;
>for whenever I was before you, my heart,
>I never worried about being blamed.
>
>If similarly I feigned so before others
>I never believed I was watched at all;
>for I bear such suffering and such pain
>that death would be more welcome than life.
>
>Whichever man loves perfectly in his heart
>has no understanding or measure,
>so ardently burns the fire of love.
>
>And if nature can be changed in any way,
>it should do so truly for lovers
>so painful and hard is their condition.

52. Or ho perduta tutta mia speranza
e non attendo mai gioia né diporto,
poi che madonna, ch'era il mio conforto,
cangiata m'ha la sua bella sembianza,

e fatt'ha co·l'Amore sua acordanza
ch'io viveraggio assai peggio che morto.
Ai dolce donna mia, pensa che torto
hai di mia greve e dura malenanza!

Oi gentil donna, come faraggio eo?
Dapoi che ver' di me cangiata siete,
già mai nulla allegranza non ispero.

Ma 'l fino amor ch'io porto, viso clero,
in gioia mi tornerà; come solete
sarete pïetosa, amore meo.

52. The lady behaves cruelly toward the lover, and yet he still has hope that she'll take pity on him.

> Now I have discarded all my hope
> and I don't expect any joy or distraction
> since my lady, who was all my comfort,
> has changed her demeanor towards me.
>
> And she made an arrangement with Love
> that my life will be far worse than death.
> Oh, my sweet lady, consider how wrong
> you are about my bad state, harsh and grave.
>
> Oh, gentle lady, how will I go on
> since you have changed your ways toward me?
> I have no more hope of any happiness.
>
> But the fine love I still bear, bright face,
> will turn into joy, if as is your way,
> you will take pity on me, my love.

53. Lo vostro dolze ed umíle conforto
mi dà sovente gioia ed allegranza;
ond'io però la vita in core porto,
e per aver di voi ferma speranza.

Ma rea fortuna non mi lascia in porto
sì tosto giugner com'ho disïanza:
ma, tosto ch'anderà via il tempo torto,
mi riterrà madonna in sua possanza.

Da che madonna dol quand'io aggio doglia,
dovria più soferente esser del male,
poi che 'l mio ne saria ben per sua voglia.

Ed è ben sì cortese e tanto vale
che spesso si lamenta e si cordoglia,
ed ha dolor di mia pena mortale.

53. The lady has taken pity on the lover, and shares in his pains.

>Your sweetest and most humble succor
>frequently gives me joy and gaiety;
>I therefore carry my life in my heart
>since I place my solid hope in you.
>
>But cruel fortune doesn't allow me
>to arrive quickly in a safe harbor;
>instead as soon as the bad times move on
>my lady still holds me in her lordship.
>
>Since my lady aches when I feel pain
>she should be more patient with my suffering —
>I will be well only when she wills it.
>
>And she is so courtly and worthy
>that she often laments and her heart breaks,
>and suffers over my mortal pain.

54. 'Poi che voi piace ch'io mostri alegranza,
madonna, ed i' 'l faraggio volontiera.'
'Meo sire e tutta mia disderanza,
alegra lo tuo core e la tua cera.'

'O donna mïa, merzé e pietanza
dimando, se mostrat'ho doglia fera.'
'Meo sire, se ralegri sua sembianza:
già mai non cangerò disio né spera.'

'Merzede, Amor, ch'io non saccio che dire
ver' la mia donna, tanto m'è gioiosa:
tu se' il mio core, Amore, e il mio disire.'

'Oi Amador, di fin cor l'amorosa
lëalmente ama senza mai fallire,
però ch'ell'ama te sovr'ogni cosa.'

54. An amorous dialogue between the lover and the lady.

'Since you want me to show gaiety
my lady, I will do so willingly.'
'My lord and my complete desire:
make it so your heart and face are joyful.'

'Oh, my lady, mercy and pity
is what I ask if I've shown fierce pain.'
'My lord, if its appearance is joyful,
I'll never change my desire or hope.'

'Mercy, Love, for I don't know what to say
to my lady, she is so joyful with me:
you know my heart, Love, and my desire.'

'Oh, Lover, love her with a fine heart
loyally, without ever failing,
because she loves you above all else.'

55. Madonna

Oi amoroso e mio fedele amante,
amato più di null'altro amadore,
se tu ti doli, i' aggio pene tante
ch'ardo tutta ed incendo per amore.

E se lo core meo fosse diamante,
non doveria aver forza né valore;
e se di doglia in cera fai sembiante,
eo sono, eo, quella che la porto in core.

Amore meo, cui più coralmente amo
ch'amasse già mai donna suo servente,
e che non fece Tisbïa Prïamo,

l'atender non ti sia disavenente,
ched io tanto del cor disio e bramo
che picciol tempo, amor, serai atendente.

Sonnets 55–58: A *corona*, or sequence of sonnets, consisting of a dialogue between the lady and her lover.

55.   Lady

      Oh, my loving and faithful lover,
      beloved more than any other lover,
      if you suffer, I too have great pains
      so that I'm all aflame and burn for love.

      And if my heart were made of diamond,
      it wouldn't have any strength or value;
      and if you show your pains on your face
      I'm the one — me — who bears them in her heart.

      My love, whom I love with more of my heart
      than any lady ever loved her servant
      or than Thisbe ever loved Pyramus,

      waiting shouldn't be difficult for you,
      for I so yearn and desire in my heart
      that in short time, love, you'll feel fulfilled.

56. Messere

Graza e merzé vi chero e a voi mi rendo,
donna, ch'io per neiente non son degno;
l'amoroso consiglio vostro prendo,
sperando venire nel vostro regno.

E s'io aggio fallato, al vostro amendo
son, di voi, donna, mio core e sostegno;
e s'io lamento e doglio e non atendo,
ormai di più doler muto divegno.

La vostra doglia sia la doglia mia,
e la mia doglia metto 'n ubrianza;
più pene soferò ch'io non sofria:

ma non, mia donna, che paia sembianza.
Gentile ed amorosa più che sia,
a voi rendo merzé d'esta inoranza.

56. Lover

I humbly beg for your grace and mercy
lady, since for no reason am I worthy;
I accept your amorous counsel
hoping to come under your lordship.

And if I've ever failed, I'll endure
your correction, my lady and my heart;
and if I lament and if I suffer
I won't await more pain to become silent.

May your torment become my torment
and I will forget all my suffering;
I'll suffer more pains than I already suffered;

but it should not, my lady, seem mere show.
To you, most gentle and amorous,
I repay this honor with gratitude.

57.   Madonna

>Assai mi son coverta, amore meo:
>io lassa me, più non posso sofrire;
>cotanto forte d'amor son presa eo
>ch'io non aggio potenza, omè, di dire.
>
>Ch'io nonn-amo né temo tanto Deo
>quanto te, amoroso e dolze sire,
>e vo' ben che tu sacce e penzi ch'eo
>condotta son per te presso al morire.
>
>E se co·gli occhi piangi o ti lamente,
>e' son quella che non trovo riposo
>lo dì ch'io non ti veggio, amor piagente.
>
>E se due giorni o tre mi stesse ascoso,
>io n'anderei piangendo infra la gente,
>cherendo te, meo sir disideroso.

57. Lady

> For so long, my love, I've hidden myself,
> alas, that I can no longer endure;
> so strongly has Love taken hold of me
> that, oh me, I have no strength to speak!
>
> For I don't love nor fear God so much as
> I fear and love you, sweet and loving lord;
> I want you to know and believe that I,
> because of you, have been brought close to death.
>
> And if you weep with your eyes and lament,
> I am the one who cannot find peace
> the day I don't see you, my pleasing love.
>
> And if you remained hidden from me two or three days
> I would wander through the crowds crying
> and begging for you, my desired lord.

58.   Messere

Gentile ed amorosa ed avenente
cortese e saggia con gaia sembianza,
ben aggia il giorno che vostro servente
Amor mi fe', di voi che simiglianza

non avete né pare, al mio parvente.
Conforto e doglia m'è vostra pesanza,
pensandome ch'Amor veracemente
vi stringa, dolce donna, per amanza.

Di ciò prendo conforto nel coraggio,
e dolemi se voi doglia portate,
ché quando voi dolete io gioia non aggio.

Ma se di me vi pesa o se m'amate,
Amor ringrazo, che 'n suo segnoraggio
mi tene, e voi, madonn', ha in potestate.

58. Lover

Gentle and amorous and lovely,
courtly and wise and joyful appearance:
blessed be the day that Love made me
your servant, because no one resembles

or equals you, in my opinion.
Succor and torment press upon me
when I realize that Love truly
forces you too, sweet lady, to love.

I take comfort of this in my heart
and I ache if you bear any pains,
because when you suffer I have no joy.

But if I weigh on you — if you love me —
I give thanks to Love, who holds me
and you, my lady, in his lordship.

59A. Rustico to Bondie Dietaiuti:

Due cavalier valenti d'un paraggio
aman di core una donna valente;
ciascuno l'ama tanto in suo coraggio
che d'avanzar[1] d'amar saria neiente.

L'un è cortese ed insegnato e saggio,
largo in donare ed in tutto avenente;
l'altro è prode e di gran vassallaggio,
fiero ed ardito e dottato di gente.

Qual d'esti due è più degno d'avere
da la sua donna ciò ch'e' ne disia,
tra quel c'ha 'n sé cortesia e savere

e l'altro d'arme molta valentia?
Or me ne conta tutto il tuo volere:
s'io fosse donna, ben so qual vorria.

---

[1] Massèra: 'ched avanzar'.

Sonnets 59A and 59B: *Tenzone* with Bondie Dietaiuti

59A. Rustico poses the question: between a member of the low nobility, courteous and educated, and a high aristocrat, with a retinue of servants, whose love should a lady return?

> Two knights, who are equally courteous,
> love a worthy lady with all their hearts;
> and each one loves her so much in his heart
> that surpassing all others would be nothing.
>
> One is courtly, knowledgeable, and wise,
> generous in giving, and entirely pleasing;
> the other is brave, with great vassalage,
> fierce and proud, and served by retainers.
>
> Of the two of them, which is more worthy
> to have what they desire from the lady —
> between the courteous and learned one,
>
> and the other who's worthy in arms?
> Now tell me all that you want to say:
> if I were a lady, I know who I'd want.

59B. Bondie's response to Rustico[1]

Da che ti piace ch'io deggia contare
lo mio volere di ciò c'hai domandato,
diràggiotene quello ca[2] men pare,
qual d'esti due dé' essere più amato,

avvegna che ciascun sia da laudare[3]
d'alta ventura ch'a ciascuno è dato;
ma pur la donna è più degna d'amare
quel ch'è cortese e saggio ed insegnato.

Quelli con[4] fino pregio di prodezza,
tegno bene che grande onor li sia;
ma sì mi par ch'aggia maggior ricchezza

quelli ch'ha in sé savere e cortesia,
perché comprende tutta gentilezza;
s'io fosse donna, a quello m'apprendria.

---

[1] Cited from Marti (the poem is not contained in Mengaldo's edition).
[2] Buzzetti Gallarati: 'ch'a'.
[3] Buzzetti Gallarati: 'dottare'.
[4] Buzzetti Gallarati: 'ch'a'.

59B. Bondie answers Rustico's question: a lady should choose an educated man of the low nobility over a soldier of the high nobility.

> Since you'd like me to fully express
> what I'd want, about what you'd asked me,
> I will tell you whom, it seems to me,
> the lady should love between those two men;
>
> even though both of them are praiseworthy
> for the good fortune that both have received,
> it would be right for the woman to love
> the man who's courtly, wise, and learned.
>
> For the other man with his fine bravery,
> it is right that he have great honors.
> But it seems to me that greater wealth
>
> has the man with wisdom and courtesy
> because he contains all gentleness.
> If I were a lady, he's who I'd pick.

IACOPO DA LÈONA[1]

Iacopo di Tancredi was born in Lèona (now known as Lèvane). He was a notary for Bishop Ranieri II of Volterra in the 1270s. A document indicates that by March 9, 1277 he was already dead. As with Rustico, much of Iacopo's verse is dedicated to courtly love. The masterful Tuscan poet Guittone d'Arezzo lamented Iacopo's death in a *canzone*, praising his poetic skills. Guittone d'Arezzo inspired numerous followers with his *trobar clus*, a dense style marked by wordplay, equivocal rhymes (homonyms with different meanings) and derivative rhymes (rhymes derived from a common etymology), and puns. Iacopo's love sonnets show Guittone's influence, particularly poem 3, where he plays on the woman Contessa's name in his rhyme words. Iacopo dedicated one sonnet to reprehension, deriding none other than Rustico Filippi. His poetry is contained only in the manuscript Vatican Latin 3793, the same codex as Rustico Filippi's sonnets.

---

[1] Iacopo da Lèona is cited from Mario Marti, ed., *Poeti giocosi del tempo di Dante*.

1. Segnori, udite strano malificio,
che fa il Barbuto, l'anno, di ricolta:
ch'e' verso l'aia rizza tal dificio,
che tra' sì ritto, che non falla volta.

Or non è questo ben strano giudicio,
ch'a consumare ha sì la gente tolta?
Chi gli averebbe dato questo ufficio,
ch' ad ogn'om va pognendo dazio e còlta?

Non giova che la moglie l'ammonisce:
— Ché non pensi di queste tue fanciulle,
se non che sopra ti pur miri e lisce?

Que' risponde: — Perché non le trastulle?
Tôrre a' compagni non mi comparisce,
ca rimedir non posso pur le culle. —

1. Iacopo derides Rustico Filippi (nicknamed Barbuto) by presenting him as a highwayman: he's set up a military tower and exacts illicit tolls from passers-by. The reason, Iacopo indicates, is Rustico's concern with his daughters' dowries; he wants to use their marriages as a way to advance socially. Rustico echoes the concern for his daughters' marriages in sonnet 16.

>Sirs, now hear this strange way of conjuring
>income that Barbuto does throughout the year:
>for he's raised a tower in the farmyard
>and it shoots so straight that it never misses the mark.
>
>Now isn't his judgment rather strange,
>since, to ruin people, he's stolen from others?
>Who would have given him this duty?
>He charges tolls from everybody.
>
>It does him no good for his wife to warn:
>'Why don't you think about your daughters
>except to aim above yourself and preen them?'
>
>He responds: 'Why don't you amuse them?
>Robbing doesn't provide me enough —
>it doesn't even pay for their cribs.'

2.   — Amor m'auzide. — Per che? — Per ch'io amo.
    — Cui? — La bella. — E non è ella saggia?
    — Sì è. — Fai bene dunque. — Altro non bramo.
    — Se non che? — Se non lei. — Fa sì che l'aggia.

    — Como? — Servi. — Eo servo e merzé chiamo.
    — Non ti val? — Non. — Dunqu'è ella salvaggia?
    — Non è. — Che è. — Non la fere ancor l'amo.[1]
    — Dove? — Al core. — S'è d'amor loco, assaggia.

    — Varràmi? — Sì bene. — Omè, troppo tarda!
    — Non tarda. — Non? — Chéd ell'è già ripresa.
    — Di cui? — Di te. — Altro 'l mio cor non guarda.

    — Ricco se'. — Come? — Per far lung'attesa.
    — Che n'ho? — La bella. — Prima vuol ch'io arda.
    — Non vuol. — Come 'l sai? — Non fa più difesa.

---

[1] This is a prime example of an equivocal rhyme: 'amo' (I love) rhymes with 'amo' (a hook).

2. A complex dialogue-sonnet between a lover and a friend.

    'Love is killing me.' 'Why?' 'Because I love.'
    'Who?' 'The Beauty.' 'And isn't she wise?'
    'Yes.' 'Then you do well.' 'I want nothing else.'
    'If not what?' 'If not her.' 'Work to have her.'

    'How?' 'Serve her.' 'I serve her and beg for mercy.'
    'Doesn't it help?' 'No.' 'So, is she wild?'
    'She's not.' 'What is it?' 'The hook hasn't yet wounded her.'
    'Where?' 'In the heart.' 'Try to see if love dwells there.'

    'Will it be worth it?' 'Much.' 'But it's taking so long.'
    'No, it's not.' 'No?' 'Because she's been captured.'
    'By whom?' 'You.' 'My heart looks to nothing else.'

    'You're rich.' 'How?' 'Through all your long waiting.'
    'Rich with what?' 'Beauty.' 'She'd rather I burn.'
    'No.' 'How do you know?' 'She no longer resists.'

3. Contessa è tanto bella e saggia e cònta,
ch'io non lo saveria contare in conto;
contenenz' ha più gaia che si conta,
ed è accontata di ciascun om cónto.

Lo suo bel contenemento si conta
per li cónti e boni, che sanno conto:
ché pur de' cónti e de' valenti è cónta,
e d'altri che contati, non ha conto.

La contezza e 'l piacer ch'ella contène,
fa meglio contener lo più contato
e li fa far più cònta contenenza.

Contento a lei servir sta chi contène:
contar lo vi savria tal c'ha contato
ca per la sola contèn contenenza.

3. The lover's description of the lady Contessa. Clearly, however, Iacopo emphasizes his poetic skills, as the rhyme words are all derivative of her name (quatrains: conta / conto; tercets: contène / contato / contenenza) as well as two others in each line (conte / contare). He will use similar techniques in his sixth sonnet.

Contessa's so lovely, wise and adorned,
I wouldn't know how to fully narrate it:
her bearing is more joyful than has been told
and she is more kind than any renowned man.

Her beautiful reserve is talked about
by counts and good men, who know how to tell it;
because she knows even valorous counts,
and so many others they can't be counted.

The beautiful demeanor that she has
makes a man have even more nobility,
and guides him to more virtuous conduct.

Whoever's virtuous is pleased to serve her;
the man that has done so can talk about it,
because, for that reason alone, he's noble.

4.   — Madonna, di voi piango e mi lamento,
ché m'ingannate, ond'io doglio sovente.
— Messere, ed io doglio che da voi cento
fiate sono ingannata malamente.

— Madonna, per voi ho pena e tormento
e dolor ne lo core e ne la mente.
— Messere, gioco è 'l vostro ver' ch'eo sento;
per voi m'encende el foco tropp'ardente.

— Madonna, tutto avvèn per gelosia,
per fin amare, ché ciascun ha doglia,
che teme di perder ciò c'ha 'n balia.

— Messere, quel che divenire soglia
agli amadori, più fra noi non sia:
ma ciò che l'uno vuol l'altro voglia. —

4. As in the following sonnet, Iacopo composes an amorous dialogue between the lover and the lady. In this sonnet, though, he follows the same format as Rustico in sonnet 54: each interlocutor speaks for either a couplet or a complete tercet.

'My lady, I weep and lament over you
because you trick me and I suffer often.'
'My lord, I suffer one hundredfold,
since I have been cruelly tricked by you.'

'My lady, for you I have pain and torment,
and suffering in my heart and in my mind.'
'My lord, yours are joys compared to what I feel:
because of you, a blazing fire consumes me.'

'My lady, it happens through jealousy,
through fine love, because all people suffer
when they fear losing what's in their power.'

'My lord, may what typically happens
to lovers not occur between us.
What one wants, the other should desire.'

5. — Madonna, 'n voi lo meo core soggiorna.
  — Messere, e con voi lo meo si dimora.
  — Madonna, ed[1] a me lo meo mai non torna.
  — Messere, e lo meo non sta meco un'ora.

  — Madonna, che così li cori attorna?
  — Messere, è lo piager, che l'innamora.[2]
  — Madonna, sì; di voi, che sète adorna.
  — Messere, e di voi, ché bontà v'onora.

  — Madonna, dunque bene si conface.
  — Messere, sì, bellezza[3] e bontà insembra.
  — Madonna, lo vostro dire è verace?

  — Messer, di voi tuttora mi rimembra.
  — Madonna, unque altro che voi non piace.
  — Messer, morto sia chi mai ne disembra.

---

[1] Vitale omits 'ed' in this verse.
[2] Vitale: 'li "nnamora"'.
[3] Vitale and Massèra: 'bellezze'.

5. Another dialogue-sonnet between the lover and the lady. Each interlocutor speaks for a complete line.

'My lady, my heart takes refuge in you.'
'My lord, and with you does my heart reside.'
'My lady, and mine never returns to me.'
'My lord, mine doesn't stay here even one hour.'

'My lady, what is it that surrounds our hearts?'
'My lord, it is pleasure, which makes them love.'
'My lady, yes: mine loves you, you're so lovely.'
'My lord, mine loves you, for goodness honors you.'

'My lady, therefore they go well together.'
'My lord, yes, beauty resembles goodness.'
'My lady, is what you say the truth?'

'My lord, I think about you at all times.'
'My lady, I find nothing pleasant but you.'
'My lord, may whoever separates us perish.'

6. Amore par ch'orgoglioso mi fera,
tanto abbondosamente mi dà 'n costa;
più m'incalcia, che segugio[1] la fèra,
che 'n piano non la dimette né 'n costa.

Quanto partir più mi vòi da la fèra,
cotanto[2] a lei mi ristringe ed accosta;
madonna per se sola non mi fèra
cotanto male, che troppo mi costa.

E bene sape come son suo servo
e como ubedïente le son stato;
ma già l'Amore non ci pone mente.

Anzi distringe me solo, che servo:
e lei non tocca né move di stato,
e pàrtelesi da core e da mente.

---

[1] Vitale and Massèra: 'seguscio'.
[2] Vitale and Massèra: 'tanto'.

6. The lover's complaint about the cruelty of Love. As in his third sonnet, Iacopo highlights his poetic capabilities by using the same rhyme words (quatrains: fera / costa; tercets: servo / stato / mente).

>Love appears to strike me angrily,
>so harshly does he hit me in the flanks.
>He chases me like the mastiff does the prey,
>and he never leaves the hunt on plains or hills.
>
>As much as I want to leave this fierce woman,
>so she draws me in even closer to her;
>by herself my lady wouldn't do so much
>ill, but it costs me so very dearly.
>
>And she knows well how I am her servant,
>and how obedient I've been to her;
>but Love never gives it any thought.
>
>On the contrary, he only destroys me, who serve her;
>he doesn't touch her nor change her state,
>but takes me out of her heart and mind.

7. Se 'l meo 'nnamoramento e fino core
lungiamente fu tenuto ad inganno
per voi, che non curate el meo dolore
e la pena, che quasi morto m'hanno,

non è piaciuto né piace ad Amore,
però mi ristora la perda e 'l danno;
novellamente m'ha tratto d'errore
e m'ha ritornato en gioia l'affanno.

Ché m'ha da voi, mala donna, diviso
e m'ha donato a tal, ch'a sé m'accoglie
e mi dona sollazzo e gioco e riso.

Mai non m'inganneran più vostre voglie
e 'l vostro cor legger, ch'è 'n voi assiso
sì come sono in albero le foglie.

7. The traditional complaint of the lover about Love's cruelty.

>If my enamored state and my fine heart
>were treated as a deception for a long time
>by you, who don't care about my pain
>and suffering, which almost killed me,
>
>Love didn't like it nor does he like it now;
>since he restores the damage and my losses;
>he has recently corrected my error
>and has turned my torment into joy.
>
>For he has distanced me from you, bad woman,
>and has given me to one who accepts me,
>and he offers me solace, joy and laughter.
>
>No longer will your desires ensnare me,
>nor will your light heart, which resides in you
>like leaves that are attached to the tree.

8. S'i' lasciat'ho, per far mia volontade
ben'è s'io n'ho disagio, s'io nol tenni;
fare uno acquisto non è gran bontade,
ma tèner l'acquistato sol i senni.

Ché quanto l'uomo è più su, se ne cade,
tan'[1] maggiormente dice: — Mal m'attenni! —
ed io, che non poria salir più grade,
per far contegna in basso ne divenni.

Ed addivèn che per troppo savere
tolle savere ed addivèn l'om matto,
e dopo danno, patto vuol cherère.

Merzé chero, ché so c'ho troppo fatto,
che mi doniate il vostro buon volere,
ché non s'avvien d'aver voi, se non ratto.

---

[1] Massèra: 'tanto'; Vitale: 'tan'.

8. A sonnet about repentance and forgiveness.

> If, to do what I wanted, I gave something up,
> it's right that I suffer, since I didn't keep it.
> It's no great skill to acquire one thing,
> but only the wise can keep what they've gained.
>
> Because the higher the man, when he falls
> the more he will say, 'I couldn't hold onto it.'
> And I, who couldn't rise up any higher,
> because of my pride was brought so low down.
>
> And it happens that too much knowledge
> takes away wisdom and makes a man crazy;
> after he falls, he seeks an agreement.
>
> I beg mercy, for I know I've done too much
> for you to give me your good will, because
> I won't regain your good will, if not right away.

MINO DA COLLE[1]

Little is known about Mino da Colle's biography. He authored an *Ars dictaminis* about writing letters, and several of his Latin epistles survive. In addition, he composed two sonnets, one of which was part of a *tenzone*, or exchange. His respondent Monaldo da Sofena died in 1293, providing only a general date for Mino's life. Mino's sonnets appear in the manuscript Vatican Latin 3793. His penchant for wordplay suggests links with the poetry of Iacopo da Lèona, and the influence of the masterful poet Guittone d'Arezzo.

[1] Mino da Colle is cited from Mario Marti, ed., *Poeti giocosi del tempo di Dante* (Milan: Rizzoli, 1956).

1. A buona se' condotto, ser Chiavello,
se tu favelli a posta di Durazzo;
ma far lo ti conviene, ché chiav'ello
porta d'ogn'om, che di sé no' è durazzo.

D'este parole eo so ch'io t'acchiavello;
risponda lo tuo senno non durazzo,
ché altrettanto, n'accerto chiavello,
non razzerà lo tuo caval du' razzo.

Per ciò che tu se' conosciuto, amico,
da' pro' e da' valenti frâle e vano;
sì che tu non farai chirlanda mico.

Tu vivi e vai sì come molti vano;
dici che ami, e certo tu ami co'
omo di vento; e non po' dir: — È vano!

1. It is not known who the recipient of the sonnet is, nor who is Durazzo. The point of this insulting sonnet can be summed up in its rhyme words: the names of the two individuals, Durazzo / Chiavello (quatrains); and *amico / vano* — vain friend (tercets). The sonnet seems to be part of a larger exchange with ser Chiavello, because Mino asserts his superiority as a poet with the metaphor of riding a better horse.

> You've gotten to a good point, ser Chiavello,
> if you speak in place of Durazzo;
> but you need to do it, since he bears the key
> for every man who isn't tough himself.
>
> With these words, I know, I hammer you —
> your facile wisdom should answer for you;
> since otherwise, anyone will confirm for me,
> your horse can't paw the ground where I do.
>
> Because, my friend, you are well renowned
> as frail and vain by the brave and valiant,
> so you won't win the garland from me.
>
> You live and go about as many people do:
> you say that you love; but surely you love like
> a man made of wind: you can't say that I'm wrong.

Sonnets 2A–2B: *Tenzone* between Ser Monaldo da Sofena and Mino da Colle

2A. Ser Monaldo da Sofena to Mino da Colle

Ser Mino meo, troppo mi dài in costa,
per c'hai veduto che poco ti costa;
ma fuggi pur per qual vuoi ripa o costa,
ch'io non ti giunga, se venir dé' còsta.

E del corpo ti ritrarrò una costa,
e poi dirai a li tuoi amici: — Costa
questa briga, però ch'io veggio a co' sta! —
Diranno: — Mal per te, ma a noi non costa. —

Verrai a tal, che perderai la vita;
se Dio ti scampa, baldamente vita
di ber già mai senz'acqua vin di vita.

Deo, ch'or vedess'io pur qual cagion vi t'ha
commosso, a tanto mal far t'invita!
Ma or savrai com'è la cosa, a vita.

Sonnets 2A–2B: Ser Monaldo's *Tenzone* with Mino da Colle

2A. From Ser Monaldo da Sofena to Mino da Colle. Like Mino da Colle, ser Monaldo da Sofena demonstrates a penchant for wordplay; his sonnet contains only two rhyme words (quatrains: costa; tercets: vita).

> My ser Mino, you rib me too much
> because you've seen that it costs you little;
> but yet you flee to either hill or coast
> so that I can't reach you if you should approach.
>
> I will pull a rib from your body
> and you'll say to your friends: 'This strife costs
> dearly, now I see how things really stand!'
> They'll say: 'Worse for you, it costs us nothing.'
>
> You'll come to a point where you'll lose your life.
> May God save you — plainly you avoid
> ever drinking good wine without water.
>
> God, now I should see what reasoning
> has spurred you — it calls you to do such ill!
> The rest of your life you'll learn how things stand.

2B.   Mino da Colle's response to Ser Monaldo

Oi ser Monaldo, per contraro avento
tu se' infollito e gitti penne a vento;
e puoi ben dir sì contraffatt'avvento,
in detto e 'n fatto ch'io non aggia vénto.

Ora mi dì: per tuo gridare a vento,
bene che fai? Come fa l'orsa, avvento,
quando mi voglio, buon molino a vento,
e forza tal, che te di sotto avvento.

Se gran distrette mie braccia ti dànno,
che fiar pur somiglianti a quelle d'anno,
non ne fia altro: piangerà'ti il danno.

Ché tuoi parenti ed amici, che 'nd'hanno
di te rincrescimento, dicon: — Dà no!
Non aspettar tu male, ond'io ti danno.

2B. Mino's response to ser Monaldo. Mino too demonstrates his poetic acumen in this *tenzone*, as his response only has two rhyme words (quatrains: vento; tercets: danno). Mino's sonnet illustrates the quick pass from verbal abuse to physical violence. He calls Monaldo foolish, and describes Monaldo's foolish behaviors as throwing feathers into the wind. He then moves to a threat of physical violence. The comparison he makes between a she-bear and a mill isn't entirely clear, however.

>Ser Monaldo, due to adverse events
>you're foolish and throw feathers into the wind;
>and you can well make such fictional statements,
>with words and actions, that I haven't won.
>
>Now tell me for all your shouting in the wind
>what good have you done? Like a bear, I am
>a mill in the wind when I want to be:
>with similar force I'll throw you down.
>
>If my arms give you severe beatings
>they will be like the ones you got last year
>and not otherwise. Cry over your harm.
>
>For your friends and relatives who take
>pity on you all say: 'Don't do it!'
>Don't seek out harm — I'll give it to you!

NICCOLA MUSCIA OF SIENA[1]

Facts about Niccola Muscia of Siena are unavailable. Clearly he was alive at the end of the thirteenth century; chronicler Dino Compagni corroborates Guido Cavalcanti's incomplete journey to Compostella in 1297, the subject of Muscia's third sonnet. Guido Cavalcanti (*c.* 1250–1300) was one of the most influential poets of the time, responsible in part for the philosophical examination of love known as the *dolce stil nuovo*. In the *Vita Nuova* (*c.* 1294) Dante refers to Cavalcanti as one of his first literary friends. Additionally, Guido was a member of the White faction, inspired by his dislike of Corso Donati. The subject of Niccola's two other sonnets, Lano, is unknown. The identification of Muscia's Lano with Lano del Toppo (*Inferno* 13) has been proposed, but that hypothesis cannot be confirmed. Given his expressions of passionate love for Lano, as well as the slanders of him, Muscia might represent the first openly homosexual writer of Italian literature.

Muscia's poems appear in two fourteenth-century manuscripts, Vatican Chigiano Latin L. VIII. 305, and Vatican Barberiniano 3953. Muscia was derided for his sexuality by Rustico Filippi (sonnet 29) as well as by Iacomo dei Tolomei.[2]

---

[1] Vitale treats Niccola Muscia as distinct from Muscia of Siena. Marti and Bettarini treat them as the same person. Massèra published only the third sonnet below.
[2] Niccola Muscia is cited from Anna Bruni Bettarini, 'Le rime di Meo dei Tolomei e di Muscia da Siena', *Studi di filologia italiana*, 33 (1974), 31–98.

1. Dugento scodelline di diamanti
    di bella quadra, Lan vorre' ch'avesse,
    e dodici usignuo', ch'ognuno stesse
    davant'a ·llui, faccendo dolzi canti;

    e cento milia some di bisanti,
    e quante belle donne a ·llu' piacesse,[1]
    e sì vorre' ch'a scacch'ogn'uom vincesse,
    dandoli rocchi e cavalier' innanti.

    E sì vorre' la ritropia 'n balia
    avesse quelli a cui tant'ho donato
    in parore, che 'n fatt' i' non poria,

    per lo sapere[2] che ·llui aggio trovato
    co ·la beltà,[3] che ben se li averria;
    e tanto più, quanto li fosse 'n grato.

---

[1] Marti and Vitale: 'ch'e' volesse'.
[2] Marti: 'Ché del senno'; Vitale: 'ché nel senno'.
[3] Marti and Vitale: 'con la bellezza'.

1. Muscia evokes the traditional courtly world in his praise of Lano. Like a medieval lord, the poet wants to reward Lano with courtly gifts. He even wishes he could grant Lano a heliotrope, the mythical stone that rendered a person invisible. Muscia will need to content himself with words, however, since he has no such items in his possession.

> Two hundred saucers filled with diamonds
> of highest quality I want to give Lano;
> and twelve nightingales, each one of them
> singing sweet songs before him;
>
> and one hundred thousand bags of gold coins;
> and all the beautiful ladies he wanted;
> and I wish that he defeated at chess
> any man, even without rooks and bishops.
>
> And I wish he had the heliotrope —
> this man to whom I've given so much
> in words, since I can't give him the real things.
>
> Because of the wisdom I've found in him
> along with his beauty, which goes well with it,
> I'd give him even more, whatever he liked.

2. Giùgiale di quaresima a l'uscita
e sùcina fra l'entrar di fevra[i]o
e mandorle novelle di gennaio
mandar vorre' io a Lano, ch'è gioi compita:

ch'i' l'amo più che nessun uom la vita,
ed e' mi tien per suo, e·ssono e·ppaio,
ed e' se ne potrebbe aveder naio;
e a ·llui vado com' la calamita

va a lo ferro, ch'è naturaldade.
Amor comanda, e così vòl che ·ssia,
ched i' faccia per la sua gran beltade,

ch'è tanta, che contar non si poria,
ma non dico così de la bontade
né del senno, perciò ch'i' mentiria.

2. As before Muscia wishes to bestow gifts upon Lano; however, in this sonnet the gifts are not naturally available (e.g., dates in February, and almonds in January). These 'unnatural gifts' stand in stark contrast to Muscia's love for Lano, which is quite natural. With this sonnet, Muscia seems to argue against the cultural definition of sodomy as a 'crime against nature'.

>Red dates at the close of Lenten time
>and plums at the start of February,
>and fresh almonds in January
>are what I'd send to Lano, my complete joy.
>
>Since I love him more than anyone loves life,
>and he keeps me as his, as I am and seem;
>and even a blind man can see that.
>And I'm drawn to him like a magnet
>
>draws iron, which is most natural.
>Love commands it, and so may it be.
>I do this because of his great beauty,
>
>which is so great it can't be talked about.
>But I can't even speak about his goodness
>or wisdom, for whatever I said would fail.

3. Muscia derides Guido Cavalcanti (d. 1300) for not completing a pilgrimage to Compostella in 1297. Muscia describes Guido as a camel, an animal which was believed to journey only as far as it was accustomed, and then it would stop or turn back. In the thirteenth century Guido was renowned as a poet and philosopher, as well as Dante's 'first friend'. Because of his adherence to Averroism, many people considered him an unbeliever (e.g., *Inferno* 10), and Muscia may allude to this notion by stressing his failure to fulfill his religious vow to Saint James. Muscia compares him to a goose, which was a symbol of the false religious. Guido was also a member of the White Guelph faction, according to Dino Compagni, because of his hatred for the leader of the Blacks, Corso Donati. The Cavalcanti were powerful non-noble merchants, a fact that Muscia alludes to by mentioning Guido's sale of canvasses and his position as the steward of the Rusticacci. Thus, party politics may have played a part in Muscia's castigation of Cavalcanti.

Because it adds to the background of the sonnet, the passage from Dino Compagni is cited in full:

> There was a young nobleman named Guido, the son of the noble knight messer Cavalcante Cavalcanti; he was courtly and bold, but scornful, solitary and studious. He was an enemy of messer Corso and had often thought of harming him. Messer Corso feared him greatly, for he knew that he was very spirited; he tried to have Guido murdered while on a pilgrimage to Santiago de Compostella, but this was not carried out. Because of this, when Guido returned to Florence and learned of the plot, he stirred up against messer Corso many youths who promised to support him. And riding one day with some of the Cerchi household, with a dart in hand he spurred his horse against Messer Corso, believing that the Cerchi would follow him and be drawn into the quarrel. As his horse ran past, he let fly the dart, which missed. There with Messer Corso were his son Simone, a strong and brave youth, and Cecchino de' Bardi, and many others with their swords. They chased Guido but failed to catch him; they threw stones at him, and stones were thrown at him from the windows so that he was wounded in the hand.[1]

---

[1] Daniel E. Bornstein, trans., *Dino Compagni's Chronicle of Florence* (Philadelphia: University of Pennsylvania Press, 1995), Book 1, chapter 20, p. 23.

3. Ècci venuto Guido ['n] Campastello
 o ha·rrecato a vender canovacci?
 Ch'e' va com'oca, e càscali 'l mantello,
 ben par ch'e'·ssia fattor de' Rusticacci.

 È in bando di Firenze, od è rubello,
 o dòttasi che 'l popol no·l ne cacci?
 Ben par ch'e' sappia torni del camello,
 ché·ss'è partito sanza dicer: — Vàcci! —[1]

 Sa·Iacopo sdegnò quando l'udìo,
 ed egli stesso si fece malato,
 ma dice pur che non v'era botìo.

 E quando fu a·nNimisi arrenato
 vendè [e] cavalli, e no·lli diè per Dio,
 e trassesi li sproni ed è albergato.

---

[1] Massèra and Marti read this sonnet as a dialogue, with the quatrains being the utterance of one speaker, and the tercets being the response of another.

Has Guido come to Compostella
or did he stop to sell canvasses?
He goes like a goose and his mantle falls off,
and he seems the Rusticaccis' steward.

Is he banished from Florence, or a rebel?
Does he fear that people will chase him off?
It seems he knows well how a camel turns back,
for he left without saying: 'Giddy-up!'

Saint James disdained when he heard the news,
and he, too, claims to have fallen ill;
but still he claims that he took no oath.

And when he finally arrived in Nîmes
he sold his horses but gave nothing to God —
he removed his spurs and retired to an inn.

IACOMO DE' TOLOMEI, NICKNAMED 'IL GRAFFIONE' ('THE LACERATOR')[1]

Iacomo di Messere Lottorengo de' Tolomei lived in Siena in the second half of the thirteenth century. He died prior to 1290. His sonnet is contained in the Trevisan manuscript Vatican Latin Barberiniano 3953 (*unicus*).

---

[1] Iacomo dei Tolomei is cited from Mario Marti, ed., *Poeti giocosi del tempo di Dante*.

1. Le favole, compar, ch'om dice tante,
    son ver per cert' e nessun le contenda:
    ch'anticamente fûr orchi e gigante
    e streghe, che andavan en[1] tregenda.

    E parlavan le bestie tutte quante,
    secondo Isòpo conta en so'[2] leggenda;
    ed ancor oggi viene 'l semegliante:
    e s'i' nol provo, vo' che l'om me penda.

    Ser Lici è orco e mangia li garzone,
    e 'l Muscia strega, ch'è fatto, d'om, gatta,
    e va di notte e poppa le persone.

    Guglielmo de Bediera è per ragione
    Gigante, che n'è nata la sua schiatta;
    ser Benencasa parla, ed è montone.

---

[1] Massèra and Vitale: 'in'.
[2] Massèra and Vitale: 'in su''.

1. No documentation confirms the identities of Ser Lici, Guglielmo de Bediera, or Ser Benencasa. However, in this sonnet he derides the poet Niccola Muscia, who was castigated by Rustico Filippi (sonnet 29). Muscia's poetry also appears in this volume.

> Fables, my friend, that are told in great numbers
> are true, and may nobody challenge them:
> for long ago there were ogres and giants
> and witches, who traveled in great covens.
>
> And all the animals spoke, every last one,
> as Aesop narrates in all of his legends.
> Even today the same thing takes place,
> and if I can't prove it, so may I be hanged!
>
> Ser Lici is an ogre who eats young lads,
> Muscia's a witch, a she-cat in human form,
> who goes by night and suckles on people.
>
> Guglielmo de Bedera is by rights
> a giant, whose clan was sired by him,
> ser Benencasa speaks, but he is a ram.

DANTE'S *TENZONE* WITH FORESE DONATI

~

Before 1296, Dante engaged in a *tenzone* (poetic exchange) with Forese Donati, a distant relative of Dante's wife Gemma. Forese was a member of the powerful Donati family and brother of Corso, the leader of the Black faction of the Guelphs. According to legend, the Donati had played a central role in the 1215 murder of Buondelmonte de' Buondelmonti, the incident that gave rise to the warfare between the Florentine Guelphs and Ghibellines. By the 1290s, however, members of the Donati family were famous as criminals; Dante puts Cianfa and Buoso Donati, for instance, among the thieves in hell (*Inferno* 25). Forese's father, Simone, conspired with the impersonator Gianni Schicchi to rewrite the testament of an uncle after he had passed on. By the 1290s, the Donati's reputation had fallen to the point that they'd been given the nickname 'Malefami', or infamous. Despite its mocking tone, the *tenzone* is a document of the complex interpersonal relationship between its two participants. Forese died in 1296, and it was said that Dante was present at his deathbed. In cantos 23 and 24 of *Purgatorio*, Dante happily meets Forese's spirit on the terrace of gluttony, revisiting a key charge of the *tenzone*. In that episode, Dante revisits the accusations of the *tenzone*: he mentions Forese's altered face, and Forese attributes his quick ascent of the mountain to his beloved wife Nella's devoted prayers.

Dante's contributions to the *tenzone* deride Forese for his personal failings, particularly his gluttony. To pay for his food, Dante writes, Forese must resort to theivery. Indeed, Dante implicates the entire Donati clan, which has degenerated into criminality and fraud. For his part, Forese emphasizes the mercantile activities of the Alighieri in his sonnets, behaviors that were beneath true noblemen. The *tenzone* between Dante and Forese, therefore, can be read as a document of the thirteenth-century debate about nobility. Both writers pose the same question of the other: are you and your family really noble?

1.   Dante to Forese Donati[1]

Chi udisse tossir la mal fatata
moglie di Bicci vocato Forese,
potrebbe dir ch'ell'ha forse vernata
ove si fa 'l cristallo 'n quel paese.

Di mezzo agosto la truovi infreddata;
or sappi che de' far d'ogn'altro mese!
E no·lle val perché dorma calzata,
merzé del copertoio c'ha cortonese.

La tosse, 'l freddo e l'altra mala voglia
no·ll'adovien per omor' ch'abbia vecchi,
ma per difetto ch'ella sente al nido.

Piange la madre c'ha più d'una doglia,
dicendo: 'Lassa, che per fichi secchi
messa l'avre' in casa il conte Guido.'

---

[1] All six sonnets of Dante's *tenzone* with Forese Donati are cited from Dante Alighieri, *Rime*, vol. 3, *Testi*, ed., Domenico de Robertis (Florence: Le Lettere, 2002).

1. Dante to Forese Donati: Dante depicts Forese's wife as ill thanks to her meager nighttime coverings. Her threadbare coverlet is symbolic of Forese's sexual inadequacy; at the same time, its origin in Cortona, a stronghold of the Counts Guidi, suggests her infidelity as well. The Counts Guidi were a powerful and wealthy Tuscan family. As Ghibellines, they were enemies of the Guelph Donati family. In this sonnet, Dante borrows from Rustico the notion that sexual frustration results in illness (sonnets 18 and 19).

> Whoever heard the coughing of the luckless
> wife of Bicci, nicknamed Forese,
> could say that she perhaps has wintered
> where crystals are formed — in that country.
>
> In mid-August you'll find her chilly,
> imagine how she must fare other months.
> And it is no use for her to sleep clothed
> thanks to her coverlet from Cortona.
>
> The cough, the cold, and the melancholy
> don't occur because she has aged humors
> but because she feels a lack in her nest.
>
> Her mother, who has more than one pain, cries
> saying: 'Oh alas, but for dried figs
> I would have put her in Count Guido's house!'

2.   Forese Donati to Dante

L'altra notte mi venn'una gran tosse,
perch'i' non avea che tener a dosso;
ma incontanente dì ed i' fui mosso
per gir a guadagnar ove che fosse.

Udite la fortuna ove m'adusse:
ch'i' credetti trovar perle in un bosso
e be' fiorin' coniati d'oro rosso,
ed i' trovai Alaghier tra le fosse

legato a nodo ch'i non saccio il nome,
se fu di Salamon o d'altro saggio.
Allora mi segna' verso 'l levante:

e que' mi disse: 'Per amor di Dante,
scio'mi'; ed i' non potti veder come:
tornai a dietro, e compie' mi' viaggio.

2. Forese Donati to Dante: Forese responds to Dante by insulting his father, Alighiero Bellincione. Forese sees his ghost in a graveyard bound by Solomon's knot, an indissoluble knot that symbolized fealty. With this symbol he suggests that Dante's father was his eternal subject: perhaps Forese was insulting the Alighieri's lower social status; perhaps their activities as money lendors; or perhaps their economic hardships.

> The other night I had so great a cough
> because I had nothing to cover me;
> but as soon as it was day, I set off
> to go and earn wherever I could.
>
> Now hear where fortune directed me:
> for I thought I'd find pearls in a chest
> and lovely florins coined in red gold —
> I found Alaghier' among the ditches
>
> bound by a knot I don't know the name of,
> if Solomon's, or some other sage's.
> Then I crossed myself towards the east
>
> and he said to me: 'For the love of Dante
> untie me!' And I couldn't see how;
> I turned back and finished my journey.

3.   Dante to Forese Donati

Ben ti faranno il nodo Salamone
Bicci novello, e petti delle starne,
ma peggio fia la lonza del castrone,
ché 'l cuoio farà vendetta della carne;

tal che starai più presso a San Simone,
se·ttu non ti procacci de l'andarne:
e 'ntendi che 'l fuggire el mal boccone
sarebbe oramai tardi a ricomprarne.

Ma ben m'è detto che tu sai un'arte,
che, s'egli è vero, tu ti puoi rifare,
però ch'ell'è di molto gran guadagno;

e fa·ssì, a tempo, che tema di carte
non hai, che·tti bisogni scioperare;
ma ben ne colse male a' fi' di Stagno.

3. Dante to Forese Donati: Referring to Forese by his nickname, Bicci, Dante insults him for his gluttony. He's so enthralled to delicacies that he'll soon spend time in the debtors' prison across from San Simone church. Dante urges Forese to take up a new craft or else he'll end up like Stagno's sons; unfortunately, no documentation explains who these individuals were.

> You'll be tightly bound in Solomon's knot
> by roasted partridge breasts, Bicci Junior,
> but mutton loins will do far worse to you
> for their leather will avenge their flesh.
>
> You'll be even closer to San Simone
> if you don't put off your flight any longer;
> and it might already be too late
> to escape the bitter pill that awaits you.
>
> But I've been told that you know a good art
> that, if it's true, can re-establish you
> because it can bring in great earnings.
>
> And do it quickly, for you have no fear
> of your bills: but you need to laze about.
> But Stagno's sons didn't end up so well!

4. Forese Donati to Dante

Va' rivesti San Gal prima che dichi
parole o motti d'altrui povertate,
ché troppo n'è venuta gran pietate
in questo verno a tutti suoi amichi.

E anco, se tu ci hai per sì mendichi,
perché pur mandi a·nnoi per caritate?
Dal castello Altrafonte ha' ta' grembiate,
ch'io saccio ben che tu te ne nutrichi.

Ma ben ti lecerà il lavorare,
se Dio ti salvi la Tana e 'l Francesco,
che col Belluzzo tu non stia in brigata.

Allo spedale a Pinti ha' riparare;
e già mi par vedere stare a desco,
ed in terzo, Alighier co·lla farsata.

4. Forese Donati to Dante: Forese accuses Dante of hypocrisy, in that he decries the Donati's poverty while accepting gifts from the poorhouse of Saint Gall. Indeed, Dante also accepts support from the hospital in Pinti and from the Altafronti family. But, Forese claims, Dante needs to work to help his sister and brother, Tana and Francesco, so that they all don't end up poorly like their uncle Belluzzo. However, the forecast is not positive: Forese can foresee them all in the poorhouse alongside Dante's father Alighiero in his doublet, a type of undershirt.

Now go and re-clothe Saint Gall before you say
words or statements about people's poverty —
because too much pity has come to them,
this winter, who are all his dear friends.

And yet if you still see us as desperate
why do you send to us for charity?
From Castle Altrafonte you get apronfuls
so I know you are quite well-nourished.

But really, you need to go to work —
may God help Tana and Francesco —
so that you don't end up like Belluzzo.

You need to go to the hostel in Pinti!
And I can already see you at the table
and Alighiero too in his doublet.

5.   Dante to Forese Donati

Bicci novel, figliuol di non so cui
(s'i' non ne domandassi monna Tessa),
giù per la gola tanta rob' hai messa,
ch'a forza ti convien torre l'altrui.

E già la gente si guarda da·llui,
chi ha borsa a·llato, là dov'e' s'appressa,
dicendo: "Questi c'ha la faccia fessa
è piuvico ladron negli atti sui."

E tal giace per lui   nel letto tristo,
per tema non sia preso a lo 'mbolare,
che gli apartien quanto Giusep a Cristo.

Di Bicci e de' fratei posso contare
che, per lo sangue lor, del mal acquisto
sann' a lor donne buon' cognati stare.

5. Dante to Forese Donati: Dante reiterates the charge that Forese's gluttony induces him to rob. Some scholars have hypothesized that the reference to Forese's 'cracked face' indicates that he'd been branded as a thief. However, in this sonnet Dante takes aim at the degeneracy of the entire Donati clan. He questions Forese's legitimacy, explaining that he would need to ask Forese's mother, lady Tessa, about it. He also alludes to Forese's father, Simone, who lies abed fearful that Forese will be caught. Dante closes enigmatically stating that the Donati's misdeeds have corrupted their blood, so that none of their marriages are legitimate.

> Bicci Junior, son of I don't know who
> if I didn't ask lady Tessa:
> you've put so much stuff down your gullet
> that you need to steal other people's too!
>
> And now people keep a watch out for him
> with their purses at their sides as he approaches,
> saying: 'This man who has a cracked face.
> judging from his actions, is a convicted thief.
>
> And that one lies in his bed, sad about him,
> fearing that he'll be caught while robbing —
> he belongs to him like Christ did to Joseph.
>
> I'll say this about Bicci and his brothers,
> that for their ill-gotten gains, by their blood,
> they know how to be good in-laws to their wives.

6. Forese Donati to Dante

Ben so che fosti figliuol d'Allaghieri,
e accorgomene pur a la vendetta
che facesti di lu' sì bella e netta
de l'aguglin che e' cambiò l'altr'ieri.

Se tagliato n'avess'uno a quartieri,
di pace non dove' aver tal fretta;
ma tu ha' poi sì piena la bonetta,
che no·lla porterebber duo somieri.

Buon uso ci ha' recato, ben ti ·l dico,
che qual ti carica ben di bastone,
colu' ha' per fratello e per amico.

Il nome ti direi delle persone
che v'hanno posto sù; ma del panico
mi reca, ch'i' vo' metter la ragione.

6. Forese Donati to Dante: Responding to Dante's accusation of illegitimacy, Forese ironically asserts that he knows exactly who Dante's father was, Alighiero. The reason is that Dante never avenged the insults to his family. Instead, he's such a coward that he sues for peace with everyone, no matter what the affront. It is hard not to see a connection to *Inferno* 29, where Dante encounters the shade of his uncle Geri del Bello, whose murder still had not been avenged by the Alighieri. By referring to saddlebags, donkeys, and mathematical calculations on millet, Forese alludes to the mercantile activities of the Alighieri, activities considered beneath the status of the nobility.

> I know well that you're Alighiero's son
> and I learned about it from the vendetta —
> so clear and neat — that you did for him
> about the coins he changed the other day.
>
> If you'd cut someone up into quarters
> you still shouldn't have made peace so quickly;
> but now your saddlebag is so full
> that not even two donkeys could carry it.
>
> This is a fine custom you've brought, I tell you —
> whoever beats you soundly with a club
> you consider as a brother and as a friend.
>
> I would tell you the names of the people
> who belong above: but bring me millet
> so I can instead settle the account.

MHRA New Translations

The guiding principle of this series is to publish new translations into English of important works that have been hitherto imperfectly translated or that are entirely untranslated. The work to be translated or re-translated should be aesthetically or intellectually important. The proposal should cover such issues as copyright and, where relevant, an account of the faults of the previous translation/s; it should be accompanied by independent statements from two experts in the field attesting to the significance of the original work (in cases where this is not obvious) and to the desirability of a new or renewed translation.

Translations should be accompanied by a fairly substantial introduction and other, briefer, apparatus: a note on the translation; a select bibliography; a chronology of the author's life and works; and notes to the text.

Titles will be selected by members of the Editorial Board and edited by leading academics.

Alison Finch
General Editor

Editorial Board

Professor Malcolm Cook (French)
Professor Alison Finch (French)
Professor Ritchie Robertson (Germanic)
Dr Mark Davie (Italian)
Dr Stephen Parkinson (Portuguese)
Professor David Gillespie (Slavonic)
Professor Derek Flitter (Spanish)
Dr Jonathan Thacker (Spanish)

For details of how to order please visit our website at:
www.translations.mhra.org.uk

www.ingramcontent.com/pod-product-compliance
Lightning Source LLC
Chambersburg PA
CBHW071445150426
43191CB00008B/1245